Mental Illness

and Its Effects on School and Work Environments

THE ENCYCLOPEDIA OF PSYCHOLOGICAL DISORDERS

Senior Consulting Editor Carol C. Nadelson, M.D.
Consulting Editor Claire E. Reinburg

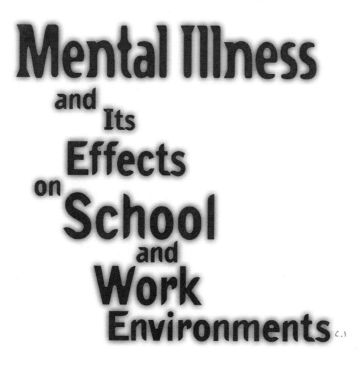

Mental Illness and Its Effects on School and Work Environments

Charles Shields

CHELSEA HOUSE PUBLISHERS
Philadelphia

The ENCYCLOPEDIA OF PSYCHOLOGICAL DISORDERS provides up-to-date information on the history of, causes and effects of, and treatment and therapies for problems affecting the human mind. The titles in this series are not intended to take the place of the professional advice of a psychiatrist or mental health care professional.

Chelsea House Publishers
Editor in Chief: Stephen Reginald
Production Manager: Pamela Loos
Art Director: Sara Davis
Director of Photography: Judy L. Hasday
Managing Editor: James D. Gallagher

Staff for MENTAL ILLNESS AND ITS EFFECTS ON SCHOOL AND WORK ENVIRONMENTS
Prepared by P. M. Gordon Associates, Philadelphia
Picture Researcher: Gillian Speeth, Picture This
Associate Art Director: Takeshi Takahashi
Cover Designer: Emiliano Begnardi

The Chelsea House World Wide Web address is
http://www.chelseahouse.com

First Printing

9 8 7 6 5 4 3 2 1

Library of Congress Cataloging-in-Publication Data

Shields, Charles.

  Mental illness and its effects on school and work environments / by Charles Shields.
    p.   cm. — (The encyclopedia of psychological disorders)
  Includes bibliographical references and index.
  Summary: Discusses mental illness, its impact at school and on the job, society's attitude toward it and those who have it, treatment options, and ways to recognize it.
  ISBN 0-7910-5318-0
  1. Mental illness—Social aspects—Juvenile Literature. [1. Mental illness.] I. Title. II. Series.
  RC454.4.S48   2000
  616.89—dc21   99-15632
                                                              CIP

CONTENTS

PSYCHOLOGICAL DISORDERS AND THEIR EFFECT

CAROL C. NADELSON, M.D.
PRESIDENT AND CHIEF EXECUTIVE OFFICER,
The American Psychiatric Press

There are a wide range of problems that are considered psychological disorders, including mental and emotional disorders, problems related to alcohol and drug abuse, and some diseases that cause both emotional and physical symptoms. Psychological disorders often begin in early childhood, but during adolescence we see a sharp increase in the number of people affected by these disorders. It has been estimated that about 20 percent of the U.S. population will have some form of mental disorder sometime during their lifetime. Some psychological disorders appear following severe stress or trauma. Others appear to occur more often in some families and may have a genetic or inherited component. Still other disorders do not seem to be connected to any cause we can yet identify. There has been a great deal of attention paid to learning about the causes and treatments of these disorders, and exciting new research has taught us a great deal in the past few decades.

The fact that many new and successful treatments are available makes it especially important that we reject old prejudices and outmoded ideas that consider mental disorders to be untreatable. If psychological problems are identified early, it is possible to prevent serious conse-quences. We should not keep these problems hidden or feel shame that we or a member of our family has a mental disorder. Some people believe that something they said or did caused a mental disorder. Some people think that these disorders are "only in your head" so that you could "snap out of it" if you made the effort. This type of thinking implies that a treatment is a matter of willpower or motivation. It is a terrible burden for someone who is suffering to be blamed for his or her misery, and often people with psychological disorders are not treated compassionately. We hope that the information in this book will teach you about various mental illnesses.

The problems covered in the volumes in the ENCYCLOPEDIA OF PSYCHOLOGICAL DISORDERS were selected because they are of particular importance to young adults, because they affect them directly or because they affect family and friends. There are individual volumes on reading disorders, attention deficit and disruptive behavior disorders, and dementia—all of these are related to our abilities to learn and integrate information from the world around us. There are books on drug abuse that provide useful information about the effects of these drugs and treatments that are available for those individuals who have drug problems. Some of the books concentrate on one of the most common mental disorders, depression. Others deal with eating disorders, which are dangerous illnesses that affect a large number of young adults, especially women.

Most of the public attention paid to these disorders arises from a particular incident involving a celebrity that awakens us to our own vulnerability to psychological problems. These incidents of celebrities or public figures revealing their own psychological problems can also enable us to think about what we can do to prevent and treat these types of problems.

Patients with schizophrenia and other forms of psychotic illness often speak of hearing voices, which they may describe as spirits or demons. In this painting, entitled "The Madwoman," Otto Dix created a sympathetic portrait of a woman haunted by such hallucinations.

THE EFFECTS OF MENTAL ILLNESS: AN OVERVIEW

What does it mean to be mentally ill? Many people know surprisingly little about this subject. According to the National Mental Health Association, a recent survey revealed the following:

- 71 percent of those participating believed that mental illness is caused by emotional weakness.

- 65 percent believed that mental illness is caused by bad parenting.

- 43 percent believed that mental illness is somehow brought on by the individual suffering from it.

In fact, *none* of these beliefs is true. All are misconceptions.

Similarly, stereotypes depicted in television, movies, and works of fiction give the false impression that most people with a mental illness are violent and likely to attack others without warning. In reality, few mentally ill individuals are violent, and with proper treatment the vast majority can become fully functioning members of society.

As many as 50 million Americans suffer from some form of mental illness in any given year. This suggests, therefore, that many families share a home with someone who is mentally ill. With mental illness so common, the prevalence of misconceptions about the condition is particularly startling.

Unfortunately, many people suffering from mental illness do so in silence. They do not seek treatment for a variety of reasons: for example, they may not be aware that treatment exists, they may believe they cannot afford treatment, or they may feel ashamed of their condition and fear drawing attention to it.

The belief that mental illness is caused by bad parenting remains a persistent and harmful myth. Parents may fail to seek treatment for a child with a mental or emotional problem, or even refuse to admit that the problem exists, for fear of being branded as failures.

Untreated, mental illness has serious effects on the individual, the workplace, and the schools. Estimates of the costs of mental illness, including both the direct costs (such as hospitalization and medication) and indirect costs (such as lost wages and caregiving time), run into the hundreds of billions of dollars. And "costs" measured in this way include only those consequences on which we can place a price tag. Think of the anguish and isolation suffered by people with a mental illness. Think, too, of the strain on family relationships and on friendships. Think of the untapped potential of students whose academic performance is affected by untreated mental illness.

Research has produced effective treatments for mental illness. Many involve various types of psychotherapy ("talk" therapy). Some treatments draw on a wide range of prescription medications. Recent developments in medical research are providing experts with an even better understanding of how the brain works and what happens when something goes wrong. As the implications of these findings are explored, better treatments will become available to people suffering from mental illness.

Contemporary society faces the challenge of recognizing the seriousness of mental illness, removing the stigma attached to the condition, and providing adequate care not only for those who suffer from it but for their families as well. The following chapters explore these issues.

In 1999, Elaine Wilson (left) and Lois Curtis were plaintiffs in a case before the U.S. Supreme Court. They contended that the Americans with Disabilities Act requires states to place mentally disabled patients in community settings rather than in hospitals. Lawsuits such as theirs challenge assumptions about the ability of the mentally ill to live and function in society.

1

WHAT IS MENTAL ILLNESS?

"Until the police took him away, he lived in a basement shoe box of a room in Queens," read a front-page story by N. R. Kleinfield and Kit R. Roane in the January 11, 1999, edition of the *New York Times*. The article told the story of a 29-year-old mentally ill man who was accused of murder.

"He would prattle on about becoming a business executive," the piece continued, "though he never progressed beyond landing a job at a Dunkin' Donuts that lasted one day. He yearned to have an adoring wife and family, but he had no real friends." Shown in a photograph being hustled away by officers, the suspect was described as "forlorn and rootless, an uncomfortable and frustrated man in the grip of schizophrenia."

Such stories about people with mental illness surface regularly. Mental illness is depicted as frightening, something to be avoided, something to be ashamed of. However, the *New York Times* article included the following statements as well: "When someone with a mental illness kills, images are evoked of a crazed and wicked population that should be separated from the rest of society, even though research confirms that the mentally ill are no more dangerous than anyone else. But many need more care than they get."

What are the facts about mental illness? What are its symptoms? How many people suffer from it and how many get help?

SOME FACTS ABOUT MENTAL ILLNESS

People who suffer from mental illness often feel that their problems set them apart as different from the rest of society in a negative way. According to the American Psychiatric Association, however, during any one year as many as 50 million Americans—close to one-quarter of the entire U.S. population—suffer from a mental disorder that interferes with work, school attendance, or daily life.

The National Alliance for the Mentally Ill points out that mental illness is more common than cancer, diabetes, or heart disease, and the World Health Organization reports that depression is the leading cause of disability in the United States.

Here are some additional facts about the scope of mental illness:

- The Center for Mental Health Services, a U.S. government agency, reports that an estimated 7.7 to 12.8 million children suffer from mental disorders, causing severe emotional or behavioral problems that significantly interfere with their daily functioning.

- At least two-thirds of elderly nursing home residents have been diagnosed with such mental disorders as major depression, according to the National Institute of Mental Health. Nearly one-fourth of the elderly people identified as senile actually suffer from some form of mental illness that can be effectively treated.

- The National Alliance for the Mentally Ill and Public Citizens Health Research Group report that 14 percent of all prison inmates suffer from schizophrenia, bipolar disorder, or major depression.

- Two-thirds of all people with AIDS will develop psychiatric problems, according to the Mental Health Liaison Group.

- Nearly all of the 31,000 Americans who commit suicide each year are believed to have a mental disorder. According to the American Psychiatric Association, suicide is the third leading cause of death among people between the ages of 15 and 24 in the United States.

- The American Psychiatric Association also reports that only 1 in 5 people with a mental illness seeks help, even though new treatments that relieve symptoms for the great majority of sufferers are available. The association estimates that as many as 8 out of 10 mentally ill people can return to productive lives if they receive appropriate treatment.

Mental illness is, in sum, much more common than many people think, and in most cases there are good methods of treating it.

According to the National Institute of Mental Health, at least two-thirds of elderly nursing home residents have been diagnosed with mental disorders such as depression and as many as one-quarter of elderly persons described as senile may actually suffer from treatable mental illnesses.

THE MANY FORMS OF MENTAL ILLNESS

Although the term *mental illness* routinely appears in newspapers, medical journals, and textbooks, it has a very broad definition. For convenience, the term is used in connection with every type of mental disorder, but it tends to be misleading for several reasons.

First, *mental illness* suggests that there is a clear difference between mental disorders and physical disorders; in reality, however, research shows that mental and physical disorders interact with each other and are interrelated. The two cannot be separated. The brain chemistry of a person who is severely depressed is different from that of someone who is not depressed, for example. That is a physical difference, and when medication is used to bring the brain chemistry back to normal, the person will experience an improvement in mental outlook. In the same way, a person suffering from hardening of the arteries that lead to the brain may have mental symptoms such as confusion and forgetfulness. When blood flow to the brain is improved through the use of medication, the mental complications generally decrease.

Second, *mental illness* as a term doesn't indicate the degree of severity of a particular disorder. Many people experiencing mental illness do not show any signs of it, whereas others may act confused, anxious, or withdrawn. Unfortunately, surveys show that most people believe that *mental illness* always refers to a severe disorder.

Third, the term *mental illness* implies that all causes of mental disorders stem from the mind itself. Most professionals now believe that mental illness derives from either biological factors or environmental factors or from a combination of the two:

- *Biological factors:* Mental illness can result from disturbances in the brain or other body-system chemistry. Moreover, people's genetic makeup—the genes that they inherited from their parents—may make them more or less susceptible to certain forms of mental illness.

- *Environmental factors:* Mental illness can stem from a person's physical, social, and cultural environment—including how the individual was raised, former and current expectations in his or her community, and the kinds of stress the person faces in everyday life.

When we use the term *mental illness,* therefore, it's best to think of it from a sympathetic perspective: how it affects a person. Mental illness may have a negative impact on the way someone thinks, behaves, or relates to others. Severe mental illness may prevent an individual from carrying out necessary tasks in daily life—such as caring for oneself, running a home, and sharing relationships.

Mental illnesses are described and categorized in the *Diagnostic and Statistical Manual of Mental Disorders,* fourth edition (*DSM-IV*), published in 1994 by the American Psychiatric Association. The manual classifies more than 200 forms of mental illness. Some of the more commonly known are the following:

- Anxiety disorders, including specific phobias (such as fear of heights), social phobia, panic disorder, and obsessive-compulsive disorder

- Delirium and dementia, including Alzheimer's disease

- Dissociative disorders, such as multiple personality disorder

- Eating disorders, such as bulimia and anorexia

- Learning disorders, including attention deficit/hyperactivity disorder

- Mood disorders, such as depression and bipolar disorder

- Personality disorders, such as borderline personality disorder and antisocial personality disorder

- Schizophrenia and other psychotic disorders, such as delusional disorder

- Sexual disorders

- Sleep disorders

- Substance abuse and disorders related to substance abuse

There are far too many forms of mental illness to describe in this book. For an overview, however, we can examine four major categories specified in the *DSM-IV:* mood disorders, eating disorders, anxiety disorders, and schizophrenia and other psychotic disorders.

Depression is the most commonly diagnosed mood disorder. Although it is normal to feel sad at times, people with serious depression suffer from long-term feelings of guilt and hopelessness. Many turn to thoughts of suicide.

MOOD DISORDERS

Mood disorders include depressive and bipolar disorders. Depression is the most commonly diagnosed emotional problem. Almost one-fourth of all Americans suffer from depression at some point in their lives. Four percent of the population has symptoms of depression at any given time.

People occasionally say they "feel depressed." And it's true that everyone "gets the blues" now and then. But people who suffer from serious depression suffer from more severe symptoms. Sometimes they say they feel guilty, hopeless, or useless. Some lose interest in eating, talking, or taking care of themselves. Many consider suicide as a "solution."

If these thoughts and feelings last for a long time, depression may be the cause. A physician can determine how serious a patient's condition is and decide whether it constitutes a mental disorder. Such terms as *major depressive disorder* and *dysthymia* are used to distinguish disorders of different durations and different levels of severity.

Bipolar disorder (formerly called manic-depressive disorder) is an illness in which the sufferer experiences emotional extremes. The individual may feel very sad, showing all the signs of serious depression, and then experience a mood swing that shifts him or her into abnormal excitement, or "mania." Friends and family may notice signs of hyperactivity, scattered thinking, distractibility, and recklessness. People in a manic state have been known to spend great sums of money, claim special powers, and go without sleep for days. Specialists distinguish among several types of bipolar disorder on the basis of the extent and severity of the mood swings.

Both depression and bipolar disorder respond well to psychotherapy and medication.

EATING DISORDERS

According to the *DSM-IV,* which characterizes eating disorders as "severe disturbances in eating behavior," this category of mental illness includes two specific diagnoses: anorexia nervosa and bulimia nervosa.

People with anorexia refuse to maintain a minimally normal body weight—essentially, they starve themselves to be thin. Their self-esteem depends on their remaining thin, and people with this disorder are intensely afraid of gaining weight.

People with bulimia have a similar need to stay thin to maintain their self-image. Bulimics, however, engage in repeated episodes of binge eating, after which they try to compensate for their excessive food intake by such inappropriate and dangerous tactics as self-induced vomiting, misuse of laxatives or diuretics, fasting, and excessive exercise.

Women are 10 times more likely than men to suffer from these eating disorders. Anorexia and bulimia usually occur during the teen years or in early adulthood, although the symptoms sometimes develop in younger children. Eating disorders rarely surface for the first time after age 40.

Both conditions can lead to damage to body organs. More than 10

Eating disorders usually appear during the teenage years or early adulthood and are ten times more likely to affect women than men. A young woman with anorexia will starve herself to remain thin, and even then she may still think of herself as heavy.

percent of people hospitalized for anorexia eventually die from the disorder, usually from starvation, suicide, or electrolyte imbalance. Fortunately, both anorexia and bulimia generally respond to treatment. Because eating disorders usually have a strong social component, psychotherapy sessions for these conditions often include other family members as well as the patient.

ANXIETY DISORDERS

It's normal for people to experience feelings of fear. Looking out for our personal well-being and safety demands that we take care, even feel afraid at times. But if a person worries excessively, or feels extremely anxious about ordinary circumstances in life, he or she may be suffering from an anxiety disorder.

One type of anxiety disorder is called simply "generalized anxiety disorder." Someone with this condition may fear for a loved one's safety, even though there's no sign of danger. Or "gut feelings" may cause the person to expect disaster to occur. Patients with this disorder report feeling "shaky" or "on edge" much of the time. This illness affects about 18 million Americans, taking a considerable toll on the sufferers' health.

In addition to generalized anxiety disorder, physicians recognize several other specific disorders, including phobias, panic disorder, post-traumatic stress disorder, and obsessive-compulsive disorder.

An estimated 20 million Americans—9 percent of the population—experience phobias. People who suffer from what are known as *specific phobias* are overcome by extreme fear or dread triggered by a particular object or situation. Some people fear certain types of animals, such as dogs, snakes, insects, or mice. Others are afraid of heights or of being closed in. If the "phobic stimulus" is something commonplace, the disability can be severe. Most such fears develop during childhood and eventually fade away. Those that last into adulthood, however, rarely disappear without treatment.

A broader type of phobia, *social phobia*, involves an extreme, unreasonable fear of being embarrassed in a public situation. People with social phobia intensely dread being watched while performing ordinary tasks—having a cup of coffee, boarding a bus, depositing money—fearing that they will be humiliated. Some individuals attempt to avoid all contact with other people, making it difficult for them to hold a job or go to school.

Panic disorder brings sudden, unexplained feelings of terror to between 1.5 and 3.5 percent of the population. Sufferers report believing that they are having a heart attack from fear. During such panic attacks, they may experience heart palpitations, chest pain, choking or smothering sensations, dizziness, hot and cold flashes, trembling, and faintness. Even more disturbing than the attacks themselves is the person's fear of future panic attacks.

Often panic disorder is accompanied by *agoraphobia*, which literally means "fear of the marketplace." Agoraphobics typically fear any place or situation in which escape would be difficult in case of a panic attack. People with agoraphobia typically avoid movie theaters, shopping malls, churches, and other crowded environments. They often become too frightened to leave their homes, feeling great distress if they must go out and doing so only if they have a friend or family member to accompany them.

Anxiety disorders involve irrational fears. Agoraphobia, for example, is the fear of public spaces and crowds. People afflicted with this disorder may even become too frightened to leave their homes.

Posttraumatic stress disorder develops in some people who have experienced or witnessed a traumatic event, such as military combat, violent personal assault, kidnapping, or a severe traffic accident. Months later, the person relives the traumatic experience through recurrent and distressing memories, dreams, or flashbacks. These painful symptoms can be triggered by circumstances that are similar to the original event: for example, a woman raped in an elevator may relive the experience whenever she approaches an elevator. A veteran of war in the South Pacific may have flashbacks during hot, humid weather. Estimates of the number of people suffering from posttraumatic stress disorder vary from 1 percent to 14 percent of the population.

People with *obsessive-compulsive disorder* suffer from obsessions, compulsions, or both. Obsessions are persistent thoughts or ideas that

Posttraumatic stress disorder is seen in people who have lived through violent, shocking, or deeply stressful events, such as military combat. The disorder was widely reported among veterans of the Vietnam conflict, many of whom relived their war experiences long after returning home.

the person cannot avoid. Compulsions are repetitive behaviors that the individual feels an irresistible, irrational drive to perform. Often an obsession leads to a corresponding compulsion. For example, a person may have recurrent, intense worries about germs on his or her hands; to reduce this obsessive anxiety, the individual may feel compelled to wash his or her hands again and again—perhaps a hundred times a day. People with obsessive-compulsive disorder will admit that their behavior is absurd—and that it can be disruptive to themselves and to others—but this knowledge does not stop them from having the obsession or carrying out the compulsion. In fact, they become quite upset if their rituals are interrupted. Almost 4 million Americans suffer from obsessive-compulsive disorder.

Theories about the causes of anxiety disorders range from imbalances in the brain's chemistry to childhood experiences. A genetic factor also seems to be involved—that is, people can inherit from their parents a susceptibility to one or more kinds of anxiety disorder.

Several forms of medication and psychotherapy work well in the treatment of anxiety disorders. Cognitive-behavioral approaches to psychotherapy (discussed further in chapter 5) can help the patient confront and change specific anxiety-producing thoughts and the behaviors that result from them. In addition, psychiatrists and other mental health professionals teach patients relaxation techniques for controlling anxiety.

SCHIZOPHRENIA AND OTHER PSYCHOTIC DISORDERS

Psychotic disorders, or psychoses, are typically the most disabling mental illnesses. Schizophrenia, the most well-known psychosis, is included in this category, as are such lesser-known illnesses as delusional disorder, schizophreniform disorder, schizoaffective disorder, and substance-induced psychotic disorder. According to the National Institute of Mental Health, more than 2 million adult Americans suffer from schizophrenia alone. Psychotic disorders, which tend to begin during late adolescence, affect persons of all ages, races, and economic levels.

Symptoms of schizophrenia may include confused thinking, delusions (false beliefs that the person holds to despite clear evidence to the contrary), withdrawal from normal social contacts, and auditory hallucinations (hearing sounds that don't exist). People with schizophrenia often make illogical statements. They may think that others are watching them or plotting against them.

In an article in *Schizophrenia Bulletin,* Marcia A. Murphy described her own experience with the illness:

> I began to have hallucinations. At first, I thought they were spirits; I thought I heard angels and, later, demons. Upon their arrival I felt no surprise; it seemed natural to me. I was not shocked, but was in awe. What sounded like baby angels was soothing; they sounded sweet and loving. They comforted me. But the demons were chilling, and I was terrified. Sometimes I had to go to bed with the light on [because] I was so frightened. The demons mocked and scorned me and sounded menacing. Even though the voices told me to do things, I never did what they said. Sometimes the voices came from machines. A running vacuum cleaner called me filthy names.

Symptoms of schizophrenia include auditory hallucinations, and false beliefs called delusions, such as the belief that one is being followed or persecuted.

> Laundry machines, air conditioners, cars, and motorcycles all taunted me. The flame on the gas stove also spoke. Sometimes I thought I heard footsteps of huge invisible men following me. When I read a book, the words became audible. And when I walked, my footsteps were words. As the wind blew, it whispered messages in my ears.

Symptoms of schizophrenia can appear suddenly during times of great stress. Most often, however, the illness develops gradually. At first, close friends and family may not notice the changes in the individual's personality, but as the illness progresses, the symptoms and behaviors can become frightening.

Research into the causes of schizophrenia is inconclusive. Schizophrenia is a brain disorder; however, there is some evidence that heredity plays a major role in producing the illness. It may also be triggered by such outside factors as other illnesses, traumatic events during childhood, highly stressful experiences in adulthood, or a combination of these.

Schizophrenia is usually chronic and recurrent, but it can be managed with antipsychotic drugs and therapy. Therapists can also help friends and family members understand the patient's needs. With such support, schizophrenics can live productive lives with few recurrences of their symptoms. Although people with schizophrenia must usually remain under medical care for the disorder throughout their lives, with treatment their behavior is rarely dangerous or inappropriate; most are able to work, live with their families, enjoy friends, and function well in society.

MENTAL ILLNESS MISUNDERSTOOD

It's not unusual to have a friend or family member who has sought help for an emotional disturbance. Still, surveys show that many people—even those with mental illness—know very little about it. Catherine Baulk wrote this about her own experiences:

> I knew practically nothing about mental illness. I knew that I must be ill because I was very depressed, couldn't concentrate and was having weird experiences: my thoughts would be projected as subtitles onto the TV screen and I would stand at the bottom of my garden and hear dance music and traffic screaming past, even though my garden backs onto countryside!

Not until this young woman entered a psychiatric hospital did she understand the seriousness of her illness.

One common misconception about mental illness is that it stems from a weakness or defect in character. Well-meaning people have been known to tell sufferers that they can get better simply by "cheering up" or "looking on the bright side." Mental illness is also falsely seen by many as characterized by being out of touch with reality. In fact, few mental illnesses, even the most severe and disabling, involve such direct disturbances in the perception of reality as hallucinations or delusions.

According to the National Institute of Mental Health, in a survey conducted in California 83 percent of the respondents believed that mentally ill people are dangerous. In actuality, fewer than 2 percent of mentally ill people pose a threat to anyone's safety.

USA Today reported the following misconceptions, which were revealed by a 1997 national telephone survey of 1,006 adult Americans:

- More than half of the respondents believed that developing chronic depression, obsessive-compulsive disorder, or manic depression can be avoided. Severe mental illnesses are, in truth, physiologically based.

- Approximately three-quarters of those surveyed associated schizophrenia with split personality, multiple personality, insanity, madness, craziness, and violence. Schizophrenia, although characterized by confused thinking, is not "split personality" or "multiple personality," however, and the vast majority of people who suffer from it are not dangerous.

- Many of the respondents believed that schizophrenia is caused by drug abuse (63 percent), a nervous breakdown (51 percent), poor parenting (34 percent), weak willpower (22 percent), and/or laziness or idleness (13 percent). None of these factors plays a part in the onset of the illness.

Consider, too, these survey results gathered by the National Institute of Mental Health:

- Ex-convicts are held in higher regard in society than people who have experienced a mental illness.

- When respondents were asked to list disabilities from most offensive to least offensive, they placed mental illness at the top of the list.

MENTAL ILLNESS CAN STRIKE ANYONE

When Abraham Lincoln was a young man, he was involved in an unsuccessful love affair. The woman he had been hoping to marry suddenly refused to see him any longer. Having already suffered a series of personal setbacks, Lincoln was left heartbroken and in despair by this rejection. He was inconsolable. Friends feared that he might take his own life. His condition was so serious that sharp objects were taken out of his reach. Today Lincoln would probably be diagnosed as suffering from severe depression.

As this story illustrates, mental illness is not limited to people in a certain social class, culture, profession, or region. It is not confined to young people, old people, men, or women. Academy Award-winning actor Rod Steiger, who starred in such film classics as *In the Heat of the Night* and *On the Waterfront*, has spoken publicly about battling mental illness. In a video produced by Emory University's Carter

Abraham Lincoln, shown here with his wife, Mary Todd, and their sons, Robert and Tad, suffered from bouts of depression throughout his life. After his assassination in 1865, Mary's behavior became increasingly eccentric, according to witnesses. She carried large amounts of money, heard voices, suffered from insomnia, and had unreasonable fears of fire and of being left alone. In 1875, a jury declared her insane, and she spent four months in a sanitarium. In 1975, the U.S. Supreme Court ruled that a person must be potentially dangerous before he or she can be committed to a mental hospital.

Center, in Atlanta, Georgia, he discussed how he struggled with "constant visions of failure" during his career. He feared that coworkers on his movie sets might discover that he was "weak and in pain." Similarly, Betty Ford, wife of President Gerald R. Ford, abused prescription drugs, trying to hide her emotional problems from the public. Actress Jane Fonda struggled with an eating disorder when she was a teenager.

Other well-known personalities who have sought help for mental illnesses include Tipper Gore, wife of Vice President Al Gore; Dick Clark, television personality and producer; Ted Turner, owner of Turner Broadcasting and the Atlanta Braves; Alma Powell, wife of General Colin Powell; Mike Wallace of *60 Minutes*; comedian Joan Rivers; television talk-show host Dick Cavett; and Patty Duke, the Academy Award-winning actress who wrote eloquently about her emotional problems in her autobiography, *Call Me Anna*.

Attitudes such as these discourage people with mental illness from getting help. In her article "Colder Weather," Emma Holm described her reaction when her mother suggested that she seek counseling:

> She asked if I wanted to "talk to someone." I laughed without meaning to. A new story to relate to my very few friends. I'm so cool my mom wants me to go to a shrink. But it wasn't cool. And after I was left alone at the dining room table, it wasn't funny either. My mother had dug up something I had worked very hard to bury and I hated her for it. I hated everyone.

As a result of the widespread misunderstanding about mental illness, moreover, most people are ashamed to be associated with the disorder. According to a 1998 study reported in *Science News*, about half of the parents and spouses of people recently hospitalized for severe mental ailments made some attempt at concealing the hospitalization from friends and neighbors. Why do people try to hide it? They do so out of embarrassment and out of fear of what others may think.

It is possible to change these attitudes, but it is important to recognize that they have deep roots. In the chapters that follow, we look at how societies have tried to cope with mental illness in the past; the impact of mental illness on our own society; the ways that society responds to the disorder; and current efforts to provide treatment.

Attitudes toward mental illness began to change in the nineteenth century. The idea that insanity was a single, permanent condition was gradually replaced by the classification of mental illnesses by type and belief in the effectiveness of medical treatment. This painting depicts a hospital ward for mentally ill patients in Italy in 1865.

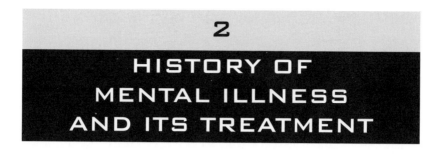

2

HISTORY OF MENTAL ILLNESS AND ITS TREATMENT

Mental illness is not a new type of disease, and the question of how to treat it is not peculiar to the modern era. As literature and historical documents show, mental illness has been part of the human story since ancient times.

Before the 20th century, such terms as *madness* and *insanity* were used to refer to mental illness. Yet what seems "mad" to one society may not seem so to another. The Greek historian Herodotus, writing in the mid-fifth century B.C., argued that King Cambyses of Persia had been mad. Why? Because Cambyses had made fun of holy services honoring the gods and had ridiculed tradition. In today's societies, especially democratic ones, such behavior might draw criticism, but it would probably not be equated with mental illness. In the opinion of Herodotus, however, Cambyses' behavior came from a mind "gone mad."

Until the 19th century, strange, antisocial behavior was thought to be the most dependable sign of insanity. Only within the last century and a half has mental illness been classified by types and causes and treated using methods similar to those used for treating physical disease. This chapter presents a brief history of mental illness that illustrates this shift from social stigma to medical treatment.

"MADNESS" IN ANCIENT TIMES

Examples from ancient history and literature demonstrate that when a person's behavior was out of the ordinary, especially if it was at odds with prevailing views of reality, the diagnosis was usually madness. In Greek mythology, the hero Odysseus, attempting to avoid service in the Trojan War, feigns madness by plowing sand instead of soil and planting salt. Similarly, in the Old Testament of the Bible (I Samuel 21:13), when David flees to Gath, a foreign land, he pretends to be mad in order to avoid being treated as an enemy. He scrabbles at doors and drools on his beard—behavior that leads King Achish to declare, "Lo, ye see the man is mad."

The power of real madness to cause harm to a sufferer was not underestimated. In Greek mythology, the god Dionysus was said to have punished Lycurgus, king of the Edonians, by turning him mad. The king seized an ax and killed his son, thinking he was chopping a vine. Similarly, Herodotus describes the mental decline of Cleomenes, a brilliant ruler whose violent outbursts became so serious that his family put him in physical restraints. Cleomenes begged for a knife, and when his keeper brought it to him, the king slashed and stabbed himself as if he were attacking an enemy.

As was the custom in both Greece and Rome, Cleomenes' family took responsibility for him. Legal means existed to prevent mentally disabled persons from ruining the family's property or finances, but institutions specializing in their care were virtually unknown. Although Roman army hospitals admitted some veterans suffering from madness, this kind of treatment was rare. More often, the insane roamed the streets and the countryside. When left unguarded, they were likely to be mistreated. People pelted them with stones or spit at them to drive them away. Nearly everyone believed that madness was contagious.

THE MEDIEVAL RESPONSE

Christianity became the official religion of the Roman Empire in the fourth century A.D., but attitudes about insanity changed very little. On one hand, the Christian emphasis on charity was of some benefit. In Russia, for instance, the notion of the "holy fool" was widespread: madmen were considered God's innocents, excused from normal behavior. On the other hand, fear of evil and demons aroused superstitions. As a result, the Middle Ages in Europe saw the rise of witch-hunts.

No doubt many of the women accused of witchcraft were mentally ill. Their crime may have been defending themselves with curses and threats. In parts of colonial New England in the late 1600s, fears linking evil with madness were also at the root of witch hysteria.

In general, the Muslim world responded sympathetically to the insane during the Middle Ages. The Islamic holy book, the *Koran,* put forth the principle that society was responsible for the weak and sick. Christian visitors to Islamic lands were astonished to find people who suffered from madness living in pleasant, supervised surroundings.

The execution of women believed to be witches was common in the Middle Ages. Many of the women burned as witches might simply have been mentally ill. A schizophrenic who claimed to hear voices, for example, might well have aroused fear and suspicion in her neighbors.

In Spain the Islamic influence inspired the founding of hospitals for the insane in the 14th and 15th centuries. In the 1540s Juan Ciudad Duarte, who had spent time in such a hospital, began a ministry that evolved into the religious order called Hospitaller Brothers of St. John of God, which built hospitals for the insane in Spain, Italy, and France. By the mid-1400s in London, too, patients at St. Mary of Bethlehem Hospital included those who had "fallen out of their wit." The cases admitted to St. Mary must have been extreme, however, because the hospital's nickname, Bedlam, became a synonym for a confusing uproar.

Overall, societies in the Middle Ages coped with mental illness poorly. In scattered locations, madmen's towers and huts offered shelter. More often, local officials forcibly expelled mentally disabled wanderers. If they returned, they were whipped. If they returned a second time, they were severely beaten. Some towns in Germany hired sailors to take mentally ill people off their hands, giving rise to the phrase "ship of fools." Where these ships went, and what happened to their passengers, is not known.

THE RISE OF INSTITUTIONS FOR THE INSANE

In the 16th and 17th centuries, civil wars rocked the foundations of Europe. Conflicts lasting decades created a governmental desire to maintain order. Enforcing the peace meant containing people who were considered to be on the edges of society—beggars, prostitutes, criminals, orphans, elderly people without means, and the insane—and large public institutions were erected to house them.

One of the most ambitious undertakings was the General Hospital in Paris, which was founded by royal order in 1656. The hospital was actu-

This eighteenth-century drawing depicts St. Mary of Bethlehem Hospital for Lunatics, which began in the fifteenth century to house people who had "fallen out of their wit." The popular name for the hospital was "Bedlam" (a shortening of Bethlehem), a word that is still used to describe great confusion.

ally a network of mental institutions or asylums, including the Bicêtre, for women, and the Salpêtrière, for men. The directors of the General Hospital were a government in and of themselves. They answered to virtually no one. They held absolute power for policing the asylums, keeping the buildings in working order, hearing difficult cases, and even feeding and clothing the inmates. The main purpose of the General Hospital was to keep undesirable people contained. Only one physician attended to 6,000 inmates. Few patients ever returned to society.

This response to the mentally ill was consistent with people's ideas about madness: Insanity, it was believed, permanently robbed people of their reason. The insane were incapable of such normal emotions as love, pride, and even pain. Because they were less than human, they could be treated inhumanely.

Asylum inmates lived in shocking conditions. Some lay naked on beds of rotten straw in cold halls infested with rats. Troublesome inmates were chained to walls, forced into cages, or beaten to "bring them to their senses." Many institutions charged admission to the public to help pay for the upkeep. During the early 18th century, thousands of visitors a year paid a penny to see the "lunatic show" at Bedlam, which was organized by inmates themselves.

REFORMS AND THE ASYLUM MOVEMENT

By the late 18th century, an intellectual revolution was beginning in Europe. This period—which later became known as the Enlightenment, or the Age of Reason—introduced the notion of scientific progress as a means of correcting social problems. Enlightenment scholars disagreed with the view that humankind must accept the harshness of the world. Instead, they proposed, science could be used to improve civilization.

In 1795 a dramatic example of Enlightenment reasoning was applied to the treatment of insanity. The chief physician of the Salpêtrière, Philippe Pinel, removed the chains from the inmates. He established the policy of substituting care and consideration for restraint. The improvement in inmates' behavior was astounding. Over time, many were released. Through observation, Pinel began to categorize types of mental disturbances, illustrating them with case studies.

Pinel's statistics revealed that insanity could be temporary rather than permanent. Mental illness was curable if diagnosed early and treated humanely. The physician Vincenzo Chiarugi had taken similar steps with inmates at an asylum in Florence a few years earlier, achieving positive results that inspired reforms in Italy. The asylum movement, as it came to be known, continued to influence the treatment of the mentally ill throughout the 19th century.

One unexpected result of the shift to medical treatment for mental illness was that middle-class people—tradespeople, shop owners, office workers—began seeking physicians' advice about ailments including such "nervous disorders" as moodiness, indigestion, and sleeplessness. A renowned Scottish physician, William Cullen, declared that many physical disorders resulted from problems with "nervous tone," or neurosis. Although psychiatry as a profession did not yet exist, Cullen's approach signaled a major change in the diagnosis of mental disorders.

By the mid-1800s, mental health had become a topic of fascination among educated people. It was fashionable to suffer from a case of "nerves," which was considered a sign that the person was intelligent, thoughtful, and sensitive. Unfortunately, an overemphasis on mental health encouraged a fair amount of quackery as well. Private asylums became highly profitable. Although some were legitimate institutions, others essentially served as resorts for the wealthy. Moreover, some asylums continued to use such harsh methods as the dunking chair, which was intended to shock the patient by plunging him or her under water.

Diagnosing and treating mental disorders became a new medical specialty. Superintendents of asylums, public and private, were professionally known as "mental alienists." The Association of Medical Superintendents of American Institutions for the Insane, which was founded in 1844, evolved into today's American Psychiatric Association.

In the 1850s, Dorothea Dix, a Boston public school teacher, became a leading proponent of improvement in the regulation of and public funding for mental institutions, lobbying state legislatures and the federal government to support these endeavors. Although Dix's efforts were not as successful as she and her allies had hoped, they helped push public attitudes about insanity into the national spotlight in the United States. Interest in treating mental disorders would surge again in the aftermath of the Civil War.

MENTAL ILLNESS IN THE MODERN AGE

The U.S. Civil War left thousands of soldiers suffering from emotional disturbances in addition to their physical injuries. Neurologists of that era, who offered advice on everything from child rearing to nutrition, were faced with bewildering cases. Most of the symptoms were

Although best known for organizing the corps of women nurses during the Civil War, Dorothea Dix (1802–1877) also campaigned for improved conditions in U.S. mental hospitals.

classified as belonging to the general category of "nervous complaints," or neurasthenia. Today many of the emotionally disturbed veterans would probably be diagnosed as suffering from posttraumatic stress disorder.

During the same era, there emerged in Germany a branch of medicine that offered a larger framework for dealing with mental, emotional, or behavioral disorders—psychiatry. At the center of the German approach was the case study. It wasn't enough for patients to describe their symptoms. Their complete life history was critical to understanding how the ego, or central self, had fallen apart. Even the unconscious—thoughts and experiences whose meanings were hidden in normal life—came under examination. Then, in 1900, a new book about the importance of the unconscious, *The Interpretation of Dreams* by Sigmund Freud, set the direction for psychiatry in the first half of the 20th century.

Freud was a Viennese neurologist who had read extensively in literature and history. According to Freud, people's waking hours provide only a glimpse of their true desires, anxieties, and fears. All human beings have fundamental needs for love, identity, security, power, and contentment. In Freud's view, the ego has the difficult job of serving as negotiator between these inner needs—many of them unconscious— and the pressures of the external world. This means that the ego is constantly trying to define and defend itself. Freud concluded that a person's mental health is associated with how well his or her ego is succeeding in this contest.

To Freud, then, mental disorders were not nonsensical behavior or

Sigmund Freud (1856–1939) believed that mental disorders stemmed from conflicts among the conscious mind, the subconscious mind, and the external world. Freud developed techniques of psychoanalysis to explore such conflicts, and his ideas were profoundly influential.

"unreason"; they were expressions of conflict. He began to develop a type of therapy—psychoanalysis—that helped resolve inner conflicts by getting the patient to recognize deeply hidden or even painful issues. Freud's research and writing revolutionized the treatment of mental illness. In the first half of the 20th century, the impact of two world wars helped speed the acceptance of psychiatry. Soldiers whose mental health was damaged by their exposure to battle provided case studies that helped physicians refine the classification and treatment of mental disorders. As psychiatry developed further as a discipline, it began to branch out into the many forms of therapeutic treatment that are available today.

By 1950, when the first edition of the *Diagnostic and Statistical Manual of Mental Disorders* provided a comprehensive summary of the latest information about mental illness, other major developments were under way in the United States:

- The number of mental health centers that offered counseling for minor mental health problems was steadily increasing. State and private hospitals were no longer the only alternatives for patients.

- Insurance companies added some coverage for mental therapy, making treatment affordable to more people.

- Rapid advances in drug therapy made it possible for patients' conditions to be quickly stabilized or improved. Tranquilizers, antidepressants, and other psychoactive drugs changed the nature of medical care. These developments allowed patients who had once been hospitalized for months or years to participate in life outside the institution. The 1960s and 1970s saw thousands of people with mental illness resume independent or assisted living with the help of drug therapy.

Today biomedical science works alongside therapeutic counseling in the treatment of mental illness. In fact, scientists are searching for genes that hold the keys to specific disorders, including alcoholism, depression, and schizophrenia. If it becomes possible to identify certain disorders by their presence in the body's genetic makeup, it may usher the dawn of a new era of treatment for mental illness.

The shooting at Columbine High School in Littleton, Colorado, in April 1999 focused national attention on all aspects of violence in schools, including the possible role of mental illness. The assumption that mental illness leads to violence can discourage students who need counseling from obtaining it, however; they may be less likely to talk about their problems if they are afraid of being labeled as "dangerous."

3

AT WORK AND AT SCHOOL: THE IMPACT OF MENTAL ILLNESS

Michael was a good worker. Then, about a year back, he began experiencing waves of anxiety that washed over him at unexpected times. Thoughts of failure and humiliation now cause him to tremble and feel short of breath. He no longer dares to attend office meetings for fear that he will be seized by an anxiety attack in front of his fellow workers. He's worried about losing his job. Even so, he's forced to call in sick a lot.

In another part of town, Althea was marking the first anniversary of her mother's death. Three months before, she had started having trouble sleeping. Then she began to arrive late for work; as she explained to her supervisor, "I feel like there's a big weight on me—I can't seem to get moving." The trouble has continued, and now, when she feels lonely at night, she drinks heavily.

At nearby Hutton High School, Gloria, a freshman, is secretly pleased with herself. After six weeks of intense dieting, she has discovered that she can go all day without eating anything. Food is under her control. In fact, she throws her meals away when no one's looking. If her parents force her to eat, she makes herself sick in the bathroom. She's vowed to become incredibly thin, even if it kills her.

And it might.

■　　　　■　　　　■

Michael, Althea, and Gloria are all struggling with different forms of mental illness. Michael has panic attacks; Althea is slipping into depression, compounded by excessive consumption of alcohol; and Gloria's extreme dieting demonstrates symptoms of anorexia. But will the people they encounter daily at work or at school recognize the extent of their problems?

Depression can be misinterpreted as laziness or a poor attitude. As a result, many students don't find the help they need or are punished for having feelings they can't change.

MENTAL ILLNESS AT SCHOOL

One of the first places where mental disorders tend to become apparent is at school. Routine tests given to children, in addition to the observations of school professionals such as teachers and psychologists, can bring to light problems that may have gone undetected by parents and physicians.

Even so, students' mental difficulties are sometimes mistakenly viewed as problems with motivation or attitude. Catherine Baulk described her school experiences in this way:

> I would try and explain to people that I was ill when teachers asked me why a particular piece of work was very poor, or my parents asked me why I had failed to produce any homework despite having sat at my desk for several hours. They just thought that I was being lazy and would angrily tell me to "stop it and pull yourself together" when I continually talked nonsense, not having any idea that I might be mentally ill.

As this account indicates, students' mental health problems can sometimes be mislabeled; they may be categorized as "bullying," "shyness," "laziness," or simply "being difficult." Instead of offering treatment, in these cases the school, the parents, and juvenile authorities often mistakenly resort to punishment in an attempt to make the student behave in a more socially acceptable fashion.

DIMENSIONS OF THE PROBLEM

The misdiagnosis of mental health problems in schools is particularly upsetting because it affects so many young people. According to the Center for Mental Health Services, as many as 1 in 5 children or adolescents may have a mental health problem that can be identified and treated.

In addition, figures provided to the center by the National Institute of Mental Health indicate that at least 1 in 10—or as many as 6 million young people—may have a "serious emotional disturbance." This term refers to a mental health problem that severely disrupts a person's ability to function socially, academically, and emotionally; in short, a serious emotional disturbance can be overwhelming. In her article "How I Cope," which appeared in *Schizophrenia Bulletin*, Tracey Dykstra described it as follows:

> My experience with mental illness began with melancholia [clinical depression] when I was 17. I remember feeling alienated, sobbing uncontrollably, and being disturbed because my mood did not match how I should feel about what was going on around me. Between my junior and senior years of high school, my sleep habits started to fluctuate wildly and I felt wholly out of control. Then I experienced my first psychotic break—thinking people could read

my mind. No one really seemed to notice I was suffering from a mental illness. My parents and other adults made comments to the effect that I was just going through my "teenage years"; however, I knew it was something more.

In spite of the large number of students with symptoms of mental illness, relatively few actually receive treatment for their conditions. According to the Children's Defense Fund, less than one-third of children under the age of 18 with a serious emotional disturbance receive mental health services.

WHAT MAKES YOUNG PEOPLE MENTALLY ILL?

As noted in Chapter 1, mental health problems can be caused by biological or environmental factors or a combination of the two. This is true for children and adolescents as well as for adults.

Examples of biological causes are genetics (the genes that we inherit from our parents), biochemical changes in the body, and damage to the central nervous system, such as a head injury. The principal environmental causes of mental health problems for young people include the following:

- Exposure to environmental toxins, such as high levels of lead

- Exposure to violence, such as witnessing or being the victim of physical or sexual abuse, drive-by shootings, muggings, or other traumas

- Loss of family or friends through death, divorce, or broken relationships

- Stress related to chronic poverty, discrimination, or other serious hardships

WARNING SIGNS

If a child is developing a mental illness, the symptoms are often visible quite early. In a *Saturday Evening Post* interview with Dr. Cory SerVass, Dr. John Nurnberger, director of the Institute of Psychiatric Research at Indiana University, noted:

It used to be thought that depression and mania didn't appear until adulthood or young adulthood. Then it became clear that you could see it in adolescents. In recent years, it's become clear that you can see depression in young children down to the age of five or

Physical abuse is a major environmental cause of mental health problems in children and adolescents. Pain inflicted in childhood leaves emotional scars that can last a lifetime.

so, and you can probably see mania as well under the age of 12, although it's much less common.

Nevertheless, to avoid being teased or criticized, young people who are mentally ill may conceal their troubles. Many students would rather suffer silently than be singled out as "weird." Vigilance on the part of parents and school officials is therefore important in order to detect potential warning signs.

Negative feelings that won't go away are one type of warning sign. Young people struggling with a mental illness often say that they feel sad and hopeless. Or they feel angry most of the time. Others cry or overreact to minor problems. Anxiety over loss of control sometimes

THE ECONOMIC IMPACT OF MENTAL DISORDERS

Although numbers can't possibly describe the distress of those who are mentally ill, they can demonstrate the overall economic impact of mental disorders on society. Citing statistics from the U.S. Substance Abuse and Mental Health Services Administration, the American Psychiatric Association estimates that the direct costs for support and treatment of mental disorders in the United States amount to $55.4 billion a year, plus $11.4 billion per year for substance abuse disorders.

These are the *direct* costs. But there are also *indirect* costs: for instance, job loss, reduced productivity, motor vehicle accidents, and an increase in the need for social welfare programs. The indirect costs far outweigh the direct costs. Based on the most recent figures—which date back to 1990—the total estimate of all costs (direct and indirect) comes to more than $273 billion per year for mental illness and substance abuse disorders.

Figures for specific illnesses are also enlightening. Data from the National Institute of Mental Health show that schizophrenia alone costs the United States about $32.5 billion annually. Clinical depression (that is, depression serious enough to be diagnosed by a physician) costs more than $30 billion a year.

How do these costs compare with those of other health-related problems facing Americans? For a fair comparison, we should look at figures from the late 1980s and early 1990s, the same years for which we considered the data for mental health. For this era, figures cited by the American Psychiatric Association place the economic impact for coronary heart disease at $43 billion per year; for AIDS, at $66 billion per year; and for cancer, at $104 billion per year. As these numbers indicate, mental illness is the most costly health-related problem in the United States.

manifests itself as constant hand washing, frustration over being less than "perfect," or unusual fears about danger to oneself or to family members.

Any major change in behavior is another warning sign. In her article "Colder Weather," Emma Holm described one such change as follows:

"If someone looked at my report card for grade ten and saw a first semester of As and one B and then Cs and one D for the second semester that person would probably say they were two different people. That person would have been right." Experiencing a sudden slump in school, losing interest in one's favorite activities, avoiding people, or having trouble sleeping because of nightmares may be symptoms of a mental health problem.

Antisocial behavior—often misunderstood as "making trouble"—is sometimes related to poor mental health. Young people who rely on alcohol or drugs, behave in ways that are life threatening, or break the law or violate the rights of others without regard for the consequences may be acting out mental hardships that need to be addressed.

MENTAL ILLNESS IN THE WORKPLACE

Young people in school are under the supervision of caring adults. But in the workplace, mental illness sufferers are sometimes merely tolerated or ignored, as long as they do their job reasonably well. Some workers, moreover—aware that they have a mental illness—learn to hide their difficulties. Why do they do so?

Many times they are afraid of losing their jobs. In spite of protections that exist under the law, bringing the problem to light can cause unwanted attention leading to what the employer may consider "reasons for dismissal." And when mentally ill people lose a job, finding a new job can be difficult. A potential employer's prejudices about mental illness can cause him or her to doubt the individual's suitability for employment.

Sometimes, too, the effects of mental illness can result in a work history that is less than impressive to a potential employer. Marcia Murphy described her experience as a job hunter with schizophrenia in this way:

> One symptom of schizophrenia is disorganization. It is true that, even though I consider myself methodical in nature, my life had been very chaotic up until 1994. I went through 20 paid jobs and 6 volunteer positions. The longest I was able to stay with a paid job was 18 months, and it was only part-time. As a volunteer, my most successful venture was working at a domestic violence shelter, which lasted off and on for 4 years.

A potential employer reading a work history such as Murphy's might well judge the applicant too unstable for consideration.

Employers have practical reasons, of course, for hesitating to hire workers with evidence of a mental illness. Businesses operate according to schedules, and absences—for whatever reason—cost them time and money. In addition, some people are uncomfortable working in the company of individuals whose behavior they don't understand. Employers have to consider such issues as cooperation among coworkers and employee morale.

FEARS ABOUT SCHOOL AND WORKPLACE VIOLENCE

In addition to the problem of trying to convince an employer that they are suitable for hire, job seekers with evidence of mental illness in their work history must face another prejudice: fears about workplace violence. In 1992 the Centers for Disease Control and Prevention declared workplace violence to be a national epidemic. In the late 1990s, in the wake of violent rampages by students at several schools across the United States, similar concerns were voiced about safety in our educational institutions.

How real are these threats? And is it people with a mental illness who are most likely to engage in these kinds of violence?

VIOLENCE IN THE WORKPLACE

Periodically, newspapers and television news programs report incidents of workplace violence: an employee seeking revenge on a supervisor, for instance, or someone taking hostages in an office building. In some cases, violence leads to murder. The FBI reports that workplace killings are the fastest-growing form of murder in the United States, accounting for more than 17 percent of occupational deaths each year.

Most people assume that such acts are somehow connected with mental illness—"some nut" bringing a gun to work. But is mental illness truly at the root of workplace violence? Should workers and employers feel put at risk by the presence of someone who has a psychiatric disorder?

One study of the question was described by Dr. Phillip Resnick at the 1996 U.S. Psychiatric and Mental Health Congress. The study found that the risk that people without a psychiatric disorder would commit a violent act at work was 2 percent over the course of a year. For people with schizophrenia, the rate of violent acts was 13 percent; for people who abused alcohol, it was 25 percent; and for people abusing other drugs, it was 35 percent. In other words, although psychiatric illness did increase the risk of violence, drug and alcohol abuse were much more significant factors than mental illness per se.

Dr. Resnick also cited the following characteristics as typical of people who engage in violent acts at work:

- The profile of a "workplace killer" is a white man in his thirties or forties. He may have lost his job or feel in danger of losing it in the near future. If he has been laid off, demoted, or fired, it was done in an insensitive manner, and he feels that it was a "dehumanizing" experience.

Police cover the body of a postal worker who wounded two people at a crowded post office before turning his gun on himself. Studies suggest that in cases of violence, alcohol and drug abuse are more significant factors than mental illnesses such as schizophrenia.

- A potentially violent employee is one who has a tendency to blame others for his or her problems, has a history of cruelty to animals, is fascinated by weapons, or has a low tolerance for frustration.

- Problems in the workplace will increase the likelihood of violence. These include chronic labor/management conflicts; frequent employee grievances; numerous injury claims, especially involving "psychic" injury; understaffing and excessive overtime; and a management style that is considered "authoritarian."

Resnick stressed that the single best predictor of future violence is a history of past violence—not a history of mental illness.

VIOLENCE AT SCHOOL

Although the publicity about violence in schools suggests that it is constantly on the rise, in some recent years it has actually declined. Regardless of the statistics, the horrific details about such incidents as the 1999 shootings at Columbine High School in Littleton, Colorado—in which two students killed 13 people and wounded 23 others before they committed suicide—have persuaded many schools to adopt stricter security measures. Even so, some parents worry about the safety of their children in school.

The roots of school violence are complex. As with workplace violence, the public often tends to assume a connection with mental illness that does not necessarily exist. Most students who are mentally ill—just like adults who are mentally ill—are not dangerous to others. If the concerns about school violence lead to, among other things, better counseling in the schools, that will be a favorable outcome. But if the concerns lead to an increased stigma attached to any child or adolescent who seems "weird" or "disturbed," that will only make it more difficult for students to receive the help they need.

In a report sponsored by the U.S. Department of Education, Kevin Dwyer, David Osher, and their coauthors emphasized three additional points relating to schools and violence:

- Most schools are safe.

- Fewer than 1 percent of all violent deaths of children occur on school grounds.

- A child is far more likely to be killed in the community or at home than at school.

■   ■   ■

Given the many concerns about mental illness at school and at work, how does society respond? As the next chapter illustrates, although our society takes steps to assist students, employees, and others who suffer from mental illness, prejudices about mental illness run deep. Schools, communities, mental health organizations, and businesses are constantly challenged to provide adequate help.

AMERICANS WITH DISABILITIES ACT:
EXPANDING OPPORTUNITIES

President Bill Clinton signs an executive memorandum on the Americans with Disabilities Act in 1998. Passed in 1990, the ADA outlaws job discrimination against people on the basis of physical or mental impairment.

4

MENTAL ILLNESS AND SOCIETY AT LARGE

L et's say a man named Jim Miller has had a heart attack. After a three-week stay in the hospital, and with the help of some medications, he returns home to his apartment. But as he comes down the stairs one morning, he runs into his landlord, who seems embarrassed. He asks Jim several times whether he'll be okay and whether he wouldn't be better off someplace where he could be "taken care of"?

When he returns to his job, Jim's coworkers behave in the same way. It's as if they think that somehow Jim's heart attack might rub off on them. They laugh uncomfortably when he calls himself "fit as a fiddle." One woman assures him that she'll always be his friend, no matter what.

The last straw is when Jim's fiancée tearfully informs him that her parents don't want her to marry someone who's had a heart attack. "Oh Jim," she sobs, "I'm so sorry."

What's going on with all these people? If this example seems bizarre, change the phrase "heart attack" to "mental illness" and you'll get a fair picture of the kinds of attitudes that many people with a mental illness must deal with. In general, society expresses sympathy for such disorders as heart disease, diabetes, and cancer. But mental illness still tends to elicit negative reactions.

Attitudes about mental illness even changed the Democratic party's ticket in the 1972 presidential election. Vice presidential candidate Thomas Eagleton withdrew his name from the ballot after major news magazines revealed that he had been treated for depression. Voters expressed concern that Eagleton might be "unstable."

THE ROOTS OF SOCIAL ATTITUDES

Why do so many people have a prejudiced view of mental illness? The basic problem is that people feel threatened by anything they see as "weird" or "crazy." Their fear also stems from the common misconception that mental ill-

Senator Thomas F. Eagleton of Missouri was the Democratic candidate for Vice President in 1972. He withdrew from the race, however, after news magazines reported that he had once been treated for depression—a condition viewed by many as an indication of mental instability.

ness is one condition: that all mental illnesses—from panic disorder to schizophrenia—have similar symptoms. As a result, they consider all people who suffer from mental illness to be equally suspect and dangerous.

The media contribute to this situation as well. As a society, we are bombarded with images of mentally ill homicidal madmen, women with multiple personalities, or homeless people who talk to themselves. We are inundated with sensational news accounts of serial killer trials in which the word *insane* (a legal term, not a psychiatric diagnosis) is used to describe suspects. Newspapers, in particular, often stress any history of mental illness in the backgrounds of people who commit crimes of violence. Television news programs frequently play up the "horrific nature" of crimes involving individuals who are mentally ill.

Fictional portrayals are even more biased. A 1997 content analysis of programming published by the American Psychological Association found that television characters with mental illnesses were highly likely to be shown committing acts of violence. In fact, mentally ill characters were 10 times more violent than the general population of television characters. Police shows, mysteries, dramas, and made-for-television movies regularly include serial killers, stalkers, and snipers who are portrayed as seriously disturbed.

The truth is that people who have mental illnesses very rarely make the news for antisocial behavior. The overwhelming majority—even those with severe disorders such as schizophrenia—want to be respected. And they would like to be free of the suffering brought on by their illnesses.

People with a mental illness are usually quite aware of the negative attitudes that others have toward them. Rather than put up with such indignities, many sufferers try hard not to be identified as mentally ill. Tracey Dykstra described the process in this way:

> In my late 20s, stressors seemed to come in rapid succession: My father died, my boyfriend and I broke up, and I lost my job. Like a soldier with battle fatigue, I just could not cope any longer. My mind seemed to spin so fast with racing thoughts that I could not carry on a conversation with anyone, and I completely withdrew from others. I knew it was only a matter of time until my family sent me to a mental hospital, so I feverishly cleaned my apartment to show them I was not totally crazy.

The strategies that Dykstra used—withdrawing from social contacts and trying her best to behave normally when other people were with her—are common among mentally ill people who fear being labeled as such. Ironically, though (as the next section shows), society in some ways helps perpetuate the mental illnesses that it views with so much disfavor.

SOCIAL PROBLEMS THAT CONTRIBUTE TO MENTAL ILLNESS

Drug and alcohol abuse in the United States is recognized as a national problem, but it is not often linked to mental illness. Actually, many people who struggle with mental illness also struggle with alcohol or drug habits. Believing that they can self-medicate the pain that accompanies mental illness, they take advantage of the ready availability of drugs and alcohol in our society. They become substance abusers, further adding to their suffering in the long run.

In the same way, people speak of stress as being a problem in contemporary American society. In most people's lives today, a substantial amount of stress is unavoidable. Because stress can aggravate the symptoms of mental illness, however, it is a greater problem for mentally ill people than it is for others. Anxiety disorders, for instance, are particularly influenced by stress. Stressful conditions may also cause mentally ill people to stop taking prescribed medications, to take the medications irregularly, or to abuse street drugs in an effort to numb their anxiety.

Poverty is another problem connected with mental illness. Limited in their work and social relationships, people with severe mental illnesses may be forced into low-paying or irregular jobs. They may end up living in poverty-stricken, dangerous neighborhoods. All too often, when they cannot hold down a job, they face homelessness. Such environmental conditions can aggravate their symptoms, causing the individuals to fall into a vicious cycle in which the poverty and the illness reinforce each other.

Finally, violence is an issue that concerns nearly all Americans. No direct link between violence and the development of specific mental illnesses has been proven. But it is well known that violence suffered in childhood—sexual or physical abuse, for example—has long-term consequences. Victims of abuse usually suffer from behavioral problems later in life, and they may pass on the cycle of violence from generation to generation. Although the violence in our society doesn't necessarily cause mental illnesses, it can clearly help trigger some conditions or worsen their symptoms.

Any discussion of the influence of violence in the United States must consider the effect of television violence. According to research conducted by TN Media and the children's cable television network Nickelodeon, in 1998 the typical child between the ages of 2 and 11 spent an average of 19.5 hours every week watching television. And Dr. Roy W. Menninger reported in 1995 that by the end of grade school, the average child has seen 8,000 made-for-television murders and 100,000 acts of violence. By the time the child reaches age 18, those numbers more than double—to 40,000 murders and 200,000 acts of violence.

Because of difficulties maintaining social and work relationships, a person afflicted with a mental illness may have trouble holding a job. Poverty and homelessness often result.

One study that Menninger cited identified a total of 1,980 episodes of violence during a single day on the television channels available in Washington, D.C.

Does watching violence on television cause young people to become more violent themselves? This is a hotly debated issue, but the National Institute of Mental Health summarizes the research in this way: "Exposure to television violence is as strongly correlated with aggressive behavior as any other behavioral variable that has been measured." In other words, the research strongly suggests that watching violence on television encourages aggressive behavior in real life.

Some researchers refer to the development of a "mean world" syndrome. Children, according to this theory, tend to believe the world really is as dangerous as shown on television. They conclude that they must protect themselves by causing others to be afraid. Although this attitude in itself does not strictly constitute mental illness, it is certainly an antisocial response that may require counseling and may contribute to the later development of other psychological problems.

The average child sees more than 100,000 acts of violence on television by the time he or she reaches high school. Research by the National Institute of Mental Health suggests that TV violence desensitizes children to real violence and encourages aggressive behavior.

SOCIETY'S EFFORTS TO PROVIDE HELP

So far, this chapter has painted a rather grim picture of the American society's attitude toward people with mental illness. It is equally important to note, however, the efforts by government, business, and schools to provide help to those suffering from mental illness.

LEGAL PROTECTION: THE ADA

A major piece of legislation that addresses the issue of mental illness in the workplace is the 1990 Americans with Disabilities Act (ADA), which prohibits discrimination based on either physical or mental impairment.

Key provisions of the act forbid an employer to ask a job applicant whether he or she has a mental disability or has been treated for mental illness. In addition, businesses must offer reasonable accommodation to employees with mental disabilities. Reasonable accommodation might mean, for example, giving the person an alternative work schedule or a quieter room to work in. It is the right of the employer, however, to ask for documentation of an illness before making changes in the workplace and to refuse to make a change if it would cause undue hardship.

To meet the provisions of the ADA, a mental disorder must substantially limit a person's major life activity. Not everyone with depression, for example, would automatically be covered under the ADA. For instance, the act's protections might not apply to those able to deal successfully with their depression—those capable of avoiding major disruptions in sleep, concentration, the ability to work with others, and the like.

EMPLOYEE ASSISTANCE PROGRAMS

One survey that was reported in *Business and Health* asked corporate leaders about the health problems they considered most damaging to their workforce. The study concluded that of the top 10 problems identified by the executives, which included stress, drug abuse, and "general mental health" difficulties, 6 could be treated effectively by trained psychologists. Backed by such studies as this, the American Psychological Association and other organizations have strongly promoted the use of mental health services by business and industry.

Many employers are getting the message. They are beginning to recognize that reclaiming good workers not only saves a company money in the long run but also improves employee morale. As a result, many businesses—including schools, hospitals, and government agencies—now offer employee assistance programs (EAPs) to help workers with difficulties, including mental illness. More than 70 percent of the Fortune 500 companies—some of the largest and most profitable companies in the United States—now have EAPs.

An EAP usually provides short-term counseling—opportunities for workers to talk to someone about their problems. Although it does not itself include a treatment or rehabilitation facility, workers are sometimes referred to outside therapists or facilities. Sometimes supervisors

FACT AND FICTION
ABOUT MENTAL ILLNESS

As chapter 1 noted, misconceptions about mental illness abound. The June 7, 1999, White House Conference on Mental Health exposed the following myths and brought out the true facts:

Myth: Mental illness is not a disease and cannot be treated.
Fact: Research has proven that mental illnesses are diagnosable disorders of the brain. Effective treatment relieves symptoms for 80 percent of people with major depression and for 50 to 60 percent of individuals with obsessive-compulsive disorder. About 70 percent of people with schizophrenia, when treated, can control such symptoms as hallucinations and delusions.

Myth: Depression can be worked through without seeking help.
Fact: Depression is a diagnosable and treatable illness. It affects 19 million Americans a year. Depression is distinguished from the sadness and mood swings that are a typical part of life in that it lasts longer and is more severe. It is the cause of more than two-thirds of the 30,000 American suicides each year. Effective treatments for depression have an 80 percent success rate.

Myth: Teenagers are just moody. They don't suffer from "real" mental illness.
Fact: About 1 out of 10 children and adolescents suffer from mental illness that is severe enough to cause some level of disruption in their lives. Without treatment, they may experience problems with schoolwork and with friends and family. They

refer employees to the company's EAP when personal problems impair job performance. But participation in an EAP does not jeopardize an employee's job security, promotional opportunities, or reputation. All records and discussions of the individual's problems remain confidential.

An EAP can typically help with such issues as job-related stress, divorce/separation adjustment, alcohol and drug abuse, parent-child conflicts, single parenting, and grief/loss issues—all of which may be may also become violent. Recent studies show that 60 percent of depressed teenagers improve with treatment.

Myth: Talk about suicide doesn't need to be taken seriously.
Fact: Suicide is the third leading cause of death among young adults. People who admit to having thoughts and plans about suicide or who have attempted suicide in the past are at increased risk for committing suicide.

Myth: We cannot afford to treat mental disorders.
Fact: Businesses and states that have plans in place to provide treatment for employees with mental illness have not experienced notable increases in expense. When the state of Ohio changed its coverage of mental illness to match its coverage of physical illness, for example, the new policy did not increase the state's costs.

Myth: People with severe, persistent mental illness cannot be productive members of society.
Fact: People with psychiatric disabilities face many obstacles. However, appropriate support services can help them to succeed. In 1995, for example, the Employment Intervention Demonstration Program of the Center for Mental Health Services conducted a study of various ways of assisting people with severe mental illness in obtaining and keeping jobs. After two years, 55 percent of the people receiving employment support services were still working.

particularly difficult for an employee with a mental illness. For more severe problems connected with mental disorders, an EAP can offer useful referrals to outside agencies.

ASSISTANCE PROVIDED BY SCHOOLS

The first stop for any concerned parent or student needing help is usually the school counselor's office. A counselor is a professional who, depending on the school district, can offer regular appointments for a

Though schools may lack the money or personnel to provide help to emotionally troubled young people, they can refer students to services in the community. Individual counseling is one of many kinds of therapy available.

student or refer him or her to other specialists in the school system, such as a social worker or a school psychologist.

Recently, some school districts have increased the level of available services. In May 1999, for example, Francis Scott Key Elementary and Middle School in Baltimore was profiled on the ABC news program *Nightline*. At FSK, as the school is known, a grant has allowed mental health therapist Melissa Grady to set up a Student Support Team, composed of Grady, a school psychologist, a counselor, a social worker, and two teachers.

The team meets every Friday to review the mental health and academic performance of all the students in the school. The six team members pay particular attention to children who seem depressed or withdrawn or whose grades have suddenly plummeted. When a student is identified as in need of help, the team sets up counseling sessions with the child and meetings with his or her parents. The counseling and follow-up activities may go on for as long as two to three years.

Most school districts do not have comparable resources available on school grounds. They can, however, refer students to a wide variety of community agencies providing such services as

- Case management (coordinating various kinds of services for the entire family)
- Counseling (individual, group, or family)
- Crisis outreach teams
- Crisis residential care
- Education/special education services
- Family support
- Independent living support
- Legal services
- Psychiatric consultation or, if necessary, in-patient psychiatric care
- Recreation therapy
- Residential treatment
- Self-help or support groups

- Therapeutic foster care
- Transportation
- Tutoring
- Vocational counseling

WHO SHOULD PAY?

The preceding pages illustrate some positive ways in which society at large has reacted to mental illness. Yet advances in treatment have often been slowed by the nagging question of who should pay for mental health services. It is much easier to agree that services should be provided than to specify who should foot the bill.

For most Americans, medical costs are covered—to a greater or lesser degree—by insurance firms. But insurance companies have not been eager to expand their policies to include mental health care. On the whole, says Kathleen Kelso, executive director of the Mental Health Association of Minnesota, "insurers would just as soon cover us from the neck down." Coverage varies from policy to policy, and the entire health insurance business is undergoing a dramatic change. In general, however, most insurance plans offer significantly less coverage for mental health care than for strictly physical problems.

In a November 1995 article entitled "Mental Health: Does Therapy Work?" *Consumer Reports* magazine reported the results of a survey of mental health care. Respondents whose insurance coverage limited how long and how often they could see a therapist—and even which type of therapist they could see—reported less satisfaction with their treatment than those whose coverage did not impose such limits. Some people, of course, pay the high cost of their own treatment. According to the survey, 21 percent of respondents cited the cost of treatment as a reason for canceling counseling sessions.

In an effort to overcome some of the insurance industry's resistance to complete mental health coverage, Congress passed the Mental Health Parity Act of 1996, which took effect on January 1, 1998. The act requires insurance companies to equalize the dollar limits that they set on mental and physical health care—both the annual limits and the lifetime totals. Although it constitutes an important first step, the act has many limitations.

The American Psychiatric Association notes that the law does not cover substance abuse, copayments, deductibles, or inpatient/outpatient treatment limits. And the National Institute of Mental Health points out that the act does not apply to businesses with 50 or fewer employees. With the large number of small businesses in the United States, some 80 million workers and their dependents are left uncovered by this legislation. Moreover, the act does not require insurance policies to include mental health coverage; it merely establishes requirements for those policies that do. And people who carry no health insurance derive no benefit whatever from the law.

Individual states have their own parity laws, but their provisions vary widely. In this still-evolving situation, an active debate continues about the best way to meet the costs of mental health care for all citizens. Addressing mental illness and promoting mental health remain major challenges for our society.

In addition to the conventional talk session between a patient and a psychiatrist, other kinds of psychotherapy are also proving to be effective. In art therapy, for example, patients can focus their minds on a calming activity and express their feelings in a medium other than words.

5

TREATMENT OF MENTAL ILLNESS

Kathy Cronkite, daughter of broadcast journalist Walter Cronkite, wondered what was wrong with her. Burdened by long bouts of sadness and anxiety, she finally visited a mental health professional who identified her problem. "The diagnosis of depression was a great relief for me," she told an audience at Emory University's Carter Center in Atlanta, Georgia. "If what I had was an illness with a name and a treatment, then I knew there was hope."

Cronkite spoke in an appearance with former first lady Rosalynn Carter and actor Rod Steiger, who has also suffered from severe depression, in a panel assembled as part of a series of presentations designed to raise awareness about treatments available for mental illness. "Mental illness can be diagnosed and treated much like diabetes or heart disease," said the former first lady, who chairs the Carter Center's Mental Health Task Force. Most mental health professionals agree. This chapter explores some of the treatment methods that inspire this confidence.

TREATMENT: AN OVERVIEW

The treatment of mental illnesses has made rapid strides in recent years. Here are a few of the highlights:

- Depression has been found to be highly treatable through a combination of psychotherapy and medication. Therapists can help depressed patients change their environment, their emotional reactions to it, or both.

- Lithium drug therapy for bipolar illness is estimated to have saved the U.S. economy more than $145 billion since 1970.

- Scientists are certain that some disorders are caused by imbalances in the neurotransmitters, chemicals in the brain that carry mes-

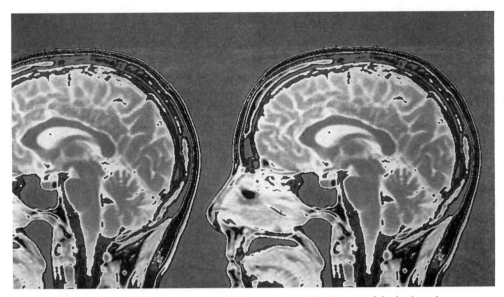

The positron emission tomography (PET) scanner provides images of the brain as it functions. Using this device, researchers have mapped the changes that occur in the brain during panic attacks and other mental disturbances. Such research is aiding the development of medical treatment for emotional illness.

sages between nerve cells. Studies have linked abnormal levels of neurotransmitters to such mental illnesses as depression and schizophrenia. Research into neurotransmitter function has sped the development of new medications, such as the selective serotonin reuptake inhibitors (SSRIs) now frequently used in treating depression.

• A technology called positron emission tomography (PET) allows medical researchers to see images of the living brain as it functions. They have seen, for example, that changes occur in certain areas of the brain when the patient is having a panic attack. Studies such as these help pinpoint the brain mechanisms involved in specific mental disorders.

• Genetic researchers, building on the knowledge that susceptibility to many psychological disorders can be inherited, are close to identifying particular genetic traits common to people with certain mental disorders. If genetic factors can be isolated, pharmacologists will be able to use that information to develop medications that are even more effective than those prescribed today.

Still, as these statistics from the National Institute of Mental Health indicate, the gap between treatment and those who need it is wide:

- Only about half of all people with schizophrenia seek treatment.

- Fewer than one-third of those suffering from anxiety disorders seek treatment.

- Fewer than one-third of those with depressive disorders seek treatment.

UNDERSTANDING THERAPY AND TREATMENT

Many people have erroneous impressions about the treatment of mental health problems. Magazine cartoons often show a patient lying on a therapist's couch, thinking out loud while a therapist takes notes. Movies also tend to give unrealistic and oversimplified portrayals: a patient is shown either in a therapist's office or in a hospital. There are, in actuality, many different settings for providing mental health care and multiple methods of treatment.

SETTINGS FOR MENTAL HEALTH CARE

Treatment for mental health problems is offered by hospitals, clinics, social service agencies, and individual practitioners:

- General hospitals sometimes have wings dedicated to treating mental disorders. There are also psychiatric hospitals devoted entirely to the treatment of mental illness.

- Working closely with hospitals is a wide variety of mental health clinics, which often have pharmacies where patients can fill their prescriptions.

- Social service agencies providing mental health care are also widespread. A school or a center for runaways might offer some of these services. A counseling center sponsored by a county or township might form part of a larger network of service-related agencies.

The exercise yard of Atascadero State Hospital in California displays two striking examples of the methods used to deal with violent mentally ill patients. The mural on the left is part of the hospital's therapy program. Above, razor wire prevents escape. Standing in the yard is the hospital's clinical administrator, Craig Nelson.

- Individual practitioners include psychiatrists, psychologists, and other licensed therapists and counselors who work from their own offices or homes.

Taking into account the full range of a community's mental health providers, a patient typically has access to many or all of the following:

- Consultation, education, and prevention services
- Daytime appointments with a specialist
- Inpatient care (including live-in facilities for patient stays)
- Outpatient care
- 24-hour emergency service

Costs for treatment at mental health facilities or by mental health professionals vary widely. They depend on the type of treatment, the therapist's training, where the treatment takes place, and the patient's insurance coverage. Some mental health professionals have sliding fees based on the patient's income.

TYPES OF PSYCHOTHERAPY

Psychotherapy, or "talk" therapy, involves talking with a therapist or counselor. Sometimes it follows the stereotypical format in which the patient lies on a couch while the therapist listens and jots down notes. Nowadays, however, there are hundreds of recognized types of psychotherapy, many of which have little to do with old-fashioned notions.

Some of the major types of contemporary psychotherapy are these:

- *Behavioral therapy* trains patients to change the behavior patterns that are causing them trouble. For instance, a person with a compulsion to wash his or her hands will learn specifically how to break that pattern. This approach typically includes stress management, biofeedback (the technique of consciously controlling involuntary bodily processes, such as heart rate), and relaxation training.

- *Cognitive therapy* helps the patient change the patterns of thinking that are causing negative feelings and behavior. When combined with the behavioral approach, this method is often called *cognitive-behavioral therapy*.

- *Family therapy* brings in members of the patient's family to address important issues that affect the entire family unit.

- *Group therapy* is usually led by a therapist, who guides the group members in discussing their personal issues.

- *Interpersonal therapy* focuses on personal relationships that cause and/or intensify the patient's symptoms.

- *Poetry, art,* and *music therapy* use art forms to help patients express their emotions and conflicts. These approaches are particularly useful with people who have trouble expressing their feelings in words.

- *Psychoanalysis* is long-term therapy that assists patients in uncovering problems and patterns of behavior that have become part of their unconscious. Recognizing these patterns

PROFILE OF A MENTAL HEALTH AGENCY: AUNT MARTHA'S YOUTH SERVICES

When you walk in the door of Aunt Martha's Youth Service Center in Park Forest, Illinois, you might get the impression that you're in some kind of school where there are no teachers and no books. Indeed, education is going on, but not the usual kind. Young people are learning to handle their mental and emotional problems. Aunt Martha's has become a model for mental health agencies across the nation.

Downstairs a dozen teenagers are in rehearsal for Project Listen, an award-winning, youth-run improvisational drama troupe whose goal is to focus adults' attention on young people's issues, such as independence and self-reliance. Upstairs are the youth drop-in center, which offers a safe, drug-free place to meet new people and make new friends, and the National Runaway Switchboard, a nationwide crisis hotline for young people.

From its inception in 1968, when a Park Forest parent voiced her complaint at a village board meeting that young people with problems needed a place to go and talk, Aunt Martha's has grown into a mental health agency that serves 12,000 children and their families per year via 80 programs offered at more than 30 sites in Illinois.

In addition to its paid staff of more than 600 employees, Aunt Martha's draws

and resolving old conflicts can help them change their current feelings and actions.

- *Psychodynamic therapy* focuses on resolving internal conflicts that are usually thought to have begun in childhood.

- *Self-help support groups* exist for all kinds of mental health concerns. Participants share their experiences and provide support and understanding for one another. Support groups can meet informally in the community or under the guidance of a therapist at a mental health facility.

With so many options available, how can a prospective patient choose? Interestingly, a study reported by Dr. Glen O. Gabbard in his on the services of about 500 volunteers. Every year, scores of new volunteers take Aunt Martha's training classes for counselors—instruction that emphasizes reality therapy, which teaches personal responsibility.

According to Nina Albrecht, development project coordinator for the agency, Aunt Martha's has two goals: (1) to protect, defend, and support children and (2) to empower them. "When things go wrong, it is extremely painful," she says. "A lot of children and parents are in pain. Aunt Martha's helps."

Tracy Swayne experienced the effect of Aunt Martha's mission firsthand. "The counselors forced me to take responsibility for my portion of my problems," said Swayne, who lived in Aunt Martha's group home for girls in Park Forest when she was in high school. Swayne, whose emotional problems seemed so overwhelming that she considered dropping out of high school, eventually graduated and went on to attend college. Now an account executive with a radio station in Chicago, she credits one of the group home parents with persuading her to take steps to change her life.

"Life is full of opportunities, and they are waiting for you," says Swayne. "Sometimes you have to ask for help."

article "Are All Psychotherapies Equally Effective?" concluded that "all forms of psychotherapy provide similar benefits. . . . A high percentage of persons who went through any type of psychotherapy benefited from it."

Basically, patients need to find a type of therapy that suits their individual needs. A person bothered by a fear of heights may not be interested in deep, long-term therapy. He or she may simply want to conquer the fear; in that case, a cognitive-behavioral approach would probably be appropriate. For a patient whose problems stem from childhood abuse, however, a psychodynamic or psychoanalytic approach might be better suited to probe the root of the trouble.

Sometimes, if a patient is involved in more than one kind of therapy, a case manager will be assigned to monitor his or her progress. Goals for

Family therapy is often combined with individual counseling. Such therapy can help family members cope with the illness of a loved one or can uncover unhealthy situations that are contributing to a patient's problems.

the therapy are set at the first few meetings between the patient and the case manager, who may be a nurse, a social worker, or a mental health worker. Regular meetings then assess whether progress is being made.

THE ROLE OF MEDICATION

Many people misunderstand the role of medication in mental illness. The popular belief is that a patient who is seriously ill must be put on drugs in order to become "normal." Actually, psychiatrists prescribe medications merely to help alleviate some of the symptoms of mental illness. When the most distracting or painful symptoms are under control, psychotherapy can be more effective. For this reason, medication is often used as an adjunct to psychotherapy.

Most medications prescribed for mental disorders affect the levels of neurotransmitters in the brain. Their mechanisms of action vary, as do the specific neurotransmitters they affect. They are divided into five broad classes on the basis of the symptoms or disorders typically treated by the medications:

Antianxiety medications. As noted in chapter 1, people with anxiety disorders experience strong feelings of tension and uneasiness, well beyond the stress reactions that most people feel. Antianxiety medications help relieve such symptoms. There are many drugs in this category. Some of the more common include lorazepam (Ativan), chlordiazepoxide (Librium), and alprazolam (Xanax).

Antidepressant medications. Antidepressant medications may be used to treat certain aspects of depression, such as feelings of hopelessness, thoughts of self-destruction, and loss of interest in life. Antidepressants restore a sense of balance in a person's outlook so that he or she can begin to address problems masked by the depression. Common antidepressants include amitriptyline (Elavil), paroxetine (Paxil), fluoxetine (Prozac), and sertraline (Zoloft).

Antipsychotic medications. Antipsychotic medications are used to treat schizophrenia and other psychoses. In lower doses they are sometimes prescribed for other mental illnesses as well. Antipsychotics tend to make patients feel better organized and more in control of their thoughts. Examples are haloperidol (Haldol), chlorpromazine (Thorazine), and risperidone (Risperdal).

Advocates for the mentally ill promote the use of medication as a way of allowing patients to lead more active lives and shortening hospital stays. Although drugs can alleviate the symptoms of mental illness, they are not a substitute for psychotherapy.

Mood stabilizers. Lithium carbonate (sold under such brand names as Eskalith and Lithane) is often used to treat certain bipolar and schizophrenic disorders, as are several anticonvulsants, including carbamazepine (Tegretol), clonazepam (Klonopin), and valproic acid (Depakene). Mood stabilizers "flatten out" highs and lows, helping the person stay on an even emotional keel.

Stimulant medications. Stimulant medications are becoming widely used for the treatment of attention-deficit/hyperactivity disorder (ADHD). Paradoxically, drugs that act as stimulants on most people have somewhat the opposite effect on individuals with ADHD. For these patients, stimulant medications can improve attention span, decrease distractibility, increase the ability to complete tasks, improve the ability to follow directions, and heighten the ability to think before acting. Stimulants used for this purpose include methylphenidate (Ritalin), dextroamphetamine (Dexedrine), and pemoline (Cylert).

Medications are prescribed for varying lengths of time, depending on the nature of both the illness and the medication itself. In some cases, patients may continue taking medication indefinitely; in other cases, the need may be brief. Ideally, medications for mental health should be prescribed only by a psychiatrist or a psychopharmacologist (a psychiatrist who specializes in medications). All doctors can write prescriptions, but specialized knowledge of the medications is as important for mental illnesses as it is for heart disease or diabetes.

ELECTROCONVULSIVE THERAPY

Electroconvulsive therapy (ECT) has been used to treat some cases of major depression, delusions, hallucinations, and life-threatening disorders. Although it has been used since about 1940, however, ECT is still controversial.

In ECT a patient is given an electric shock that produces a seizure. Although it is not known exactly what this seizure does to the brain, some studies report an 80 percent improvement in severely depressed patients. Other studies indicate that symptoms often return, even for patients who take medication.

During the 1940s and 1950s, ECT was often administered to people with severe mental illnesses. The early forms of ECT were crude, and they had many undesirable side effects. Today the shocks used are milder, and patients receive anesthetics and muscle relaxants to ease side effects. Currently ECT is administered to an estimated 100,000 people a year, primarily in psychiatric hospitals. Many researchers and physicians recommend that ECT be used only as a last resort in severe cases for which medication and psychotherapy do not seem to help.

■   ■   ■

With the wide range of options available, mental illness is indeed, as Rosalynn Carter suggested, as treatable as such physical problems as diabetes. In fact, reports the American Psychiatric Association, success rates for the treatment of mental disorders surpass those for many common medical conditions, such as heart disease. As many as 8 in 10 people suffering from mental illness are able to return to normal, productive lives after receiving appropriate treatment—treatment that is readily available in today's society.

Since leaving the White House, former first lady Rosalynn Carter has devoted much of her time to the problems of the mentally ill. She is the chairperson of the Carter Center's Mental Health Task Force in Atlanta; her book, Helping Someone With Mental Illness, *appeared in 1999. Mrs. Carter is one of many prominent people who have been treated for depression.*

The treatment of mental illness no longer takes place in remote, outdated institutions. Today many communities have their own mental health clinics or hospitals to serve local residents.

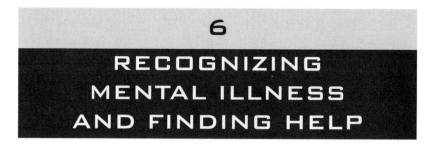

6

RECOGNIZING MENTAL ILLNESS AND FINDING HELP

Hip-hop recording artist Carl Stephenson isn't quite sure what alerted his parents to his episodes of mental illness, he revealed in an article by Mark Kemp in *Rolling Stone* magazine, "other than the fact that when you start mentioning certain things, your family freaks out and calls 911."

Actually, Stephenson's situation was not unusual. Like many other mentally ill people, he was trying to handle his problems on his own. "When I was staying with my parents," he said, "I was having these problems—like hearing voices and stuff like that. That had happened in Los Angeles, too. I was having kind of like psychic problems or what have you. So my mom and dad said, 'We want you on medications.'" After spending three years in the care of mental health specialists, Stephenson reached the point in his recovery where he could continue with his work as a musician.

Many times, friends, family members, or coworkers have to step in when a person's mental health is declining. Some of the problems discussed in earlier chapters—including negative attitudes toward mental illness and lack of information about resources—may discourage the person from seeking help. Because it can often reduce the effects of a mental illness, early treatment is vital. Therefore, it is important to be able to recognize warning signs of mental illness that call for action.

RECOGNIZING THE SIGNS

Some of the signs of mental illness commonly seen among young people are noted in Chapter 3. Here we describe the warning signs more specifically, according to how they often appear at different ages:

- In younger children, mental health warning signs include major changes in school performance, such as a decline in grades in spite of efforts at improvement. Refusing to go to bed or to go to school because of special fears—"I have bad dreams" or "No one likes me"—is a cause for concern, and such fears should be discussed with the child. Some young children, on the other hand, may not talk about their worries. Instead, they may become hyperactive and aggressive, throw temper tantrums, or deliberately disobey their elders.

- In older children and preteens, warning signs usually become more obvious. One serious problem that needs to be addressed is substance abuse. Illegal behaviors—truancy, theft, vandalism, assault—should not be dismissed as "poor judgment." These are antisocial acts that may stem from psychological problems. Sometimes the signs of mental illness are recognized best by friends and family members who know a person well: inability to cope with seemingly minor problems; complaints about feeling ill; intense fear of failure, embarrassment, or weight gain; long-lasting negative attitudes or moods; thoughts of death; frequent outbursts of anger.

- In adults, warning signs are sometimes more difficult to recognize because of the sufferer's fear of letting down family members or losing a job. The person may deny such problems as substance abuse, mood swings, excessive worries, physical ailments, and confused thinking. Elderly people sometimes say they are "slowing down," when in fact they are becoming depressed.

At any age, the following problems may disguise underlying symptoms of mental illness:

- Complaints of abuse inflicted by others

- Fears of being harmed

- Intense suspicion

- Repeated doctor's visits with complaints of flu-like symptoms, back pain, or lack of energy

- Substance abuse

Abuse of drugs or alcohol may signal an underlying mental problem, especially when it is part of a larger pattern of behavior including suspiciousness and withdrawal from friends and family.

- Threats of revenge
- Withdrawal from social situations

If you think that you or someone you know may have a mental or emotional problem, remember that mental illness is real, not a result of "weak character" or pointless complaining. The symptoms won't go away by themselves. Mental health problems need to be evaluated and treated.

WHERE TO GET HELP

Where you go for help will depend on who has the problem (an adult or child) and the nature of the problem and its symptoms. A listing of several national organizations that may be helpful to you is included in the appendix For More Information at the end of this book.

In an emergency situation, when the person or someone else might come to harm, call the police. The police are the best-trained and best-

A good first step for the student seeking help for an emotional problem is to talk to a school counselor or other concerned adult.

equipped professionals for handling violence. If the individual who caused the disturbance has to be taken to an emergency room, the next step may be admitting him or her to a hospital. This doesn't necessarily mean, however, that the person will become a long-term patient.

In a nonviolent situation, contacting one of the resources below is a good idea:

- Child-guidance counselors

- Educational consultants or school counselors

- Family physicians

- Family service agencies, which can usually be found in the Yellow Pages under such headings as "social service organizations"

- Hotlines, crisis centers, and emergency rooms
- Marriage and family counselors
- Members of the clergy

Whomever you choose to contact, describe the symptoms or problems clearly. The person you are speaking with can then suggest the type of mental health professional you should call. This professional might be any one of the following:

- A *certified alcohol and drug abuse counselor:* a person who has specific clinical training in alcohol and drug abuse
- A *child/adolescent psychiatrist:* a medical doctor with special training in the diagnosis and treatment of emotional and behavioral problems in children; child/adolescent psychiatrists are also qualified to prescribe medication
- A *clinical social worker:* a person with a master's degree in social work from an accredited graduate program
- A *licensed professional counselor:* a person with a master's degree in psychology, counseling, or a related field
- A *marital and family counselor:* a person with a master's degree and special training in marital and family therapy
- A *mental health counselor:* a person with a master's degree and several years of supervised clinical work experience
- A *pastoral counselor:* a member of the clergy with training in clinical pastoral education
- A *psychiatrist:* a medical doctor with special training in the diagnosis and treatment of mental and emotional illnesses; like other doctors, psychiatrists are qualified to prescribe medication
- A *psychologist:* a counselor with an advanced degree from an accredited graduate program in psychology and two or more years of supervised work experience

All of these professionals should be willing to provide information about their licenses, educational background, or state certificates.

Q & A: WHAT SHOULD I DO IF A FRIEND HAS DEPRESSION?

Q. What is depression?

A. Depression is an illness. It isn't a personal weakness or a character flaw. No matter how hard people with depression try to "snap out of it," they can't do so by themselves. It affects their thoughts, feelings, behavior, physical health, and appearance.

Q. Why is it important for friends and family to recognize the signs and symptoms of depression?

A. A person suffering from depression may have trouble thinking clearly. Problems may seem impossible to solve; hopelessness sets in. Depression is the number one cause of suicide. A friend or a family member must step in and help the person get treatment.

Q. What are the signs of serious depression?

A. Everyone feels unhappy now and then. But if any of the following symptoms persist for longer than two weeks, depression may be the cause:

- Feelings of sadness or "emptiness"
- Inability to concentrate or remember
- Lack of interest in such ordinary activities as participating in sports and spending time with friends
- Sudden behavior changes: taking drugs, skipping school, experiencing fits of anger

If you contact one of these mental health professionals by phone, spend a few minutes asking about his or her approach to working with patients. Is it through office visits? Group therapy? Does the person have a specialty such as child counseling, family counseling, divorce, or substance abuse? If you feel comfortable talking to the counselor or doctor, the next step is to make an appointment.

During the first visit, the doctor or therapist will want to get to know

- Physical complaints about sleeplessness or appetite problems
- Thoughts of death

Q. How can I help?

A. If it is not an emergency situation, talk to an adult you trust: a parent, school psychologist, social worker, counselor, doctor, or clergyperson. Describe the symptoms. If it is an emergency, call the police or 911.

Q. How is depression treated?

A. Depression can be treated with "talk" therapy, antidepressant medications, or a combination of the two.

Q. What if my friend is talking about suicide?

A. First, don't believe the myth that a person who talks about suicide won't go through with it. This is not true. Depression can lead, and has led, to suicide. Every year, over 2,000 teenagers kill themselves. If a friend is making such statements as "It doesn't matter—I won't be around much longer," tell an adult who will take your concern seriously. You won't be betraying your friend.

Q. What can I do to support the person?

A. Be a good listener. Don't pass judgment. Tell your friend that you understand that he or she is hurting—depression is painful. Offer your help. You may have to go with your friend to a counselor. Emphasize that you care and that's why you're involved.

the person in question. The mental health professional will ask about the problem, the person's life, and his or her family and friends. This information helps the therapist understand the situation and make recommendations for treatment.

Sometimes hospitalization is recommended. Prejudices about the shame of being "committed" to a mental institution often make family members unwilling to accept this alternative. But there may be good

The need to care for a mentally ill person can cause tension and disruption within a family. When attention focuses on the problems of the person who is ill, other family members may feel ignored or resentful.

reasons to hospitalize a family member with a mental illness, including doing so for his or her own safety. Often hospitalization allows the close supervision of medications or the initiation of a new kind of treatment. A hospital is a controlled environment where the person can receive close attention.

EFFECTS ON THE FAMILY

Most people are not prepared for the stress that mental illness places on a family. It can be very demanding both physically and emotionally. Nancy Schiller knows about caring for someone with schizophrenia. Her daughter Lori has struggled with the illness for more than 20 years. In the book *Quiet Room,* by Lori Schiller and Amanda Bennett, Nancy Schiller recalled the emotional toll on the family:

> I remember the two and a half years she lived at home after her first
> hospitalization as the most awful, stressful time I have ever lived

through. I was always walking on eggshells, always afraid I was going to do something or say something that would set her off . . . . I never slept well. I got up every night to see if she was still breathing. I would come home in the evening to find the garage doors closed and I'd be afraid to open them.

The burden of mental illness on caregivers may be far greater than previously understood. According to a survey reported in the *Mental Health Weekly* article "Study Shows Depression Prevalent Among Schizophrenia Caregivers," the mental health of many family caregivers comes dangerously close to clinical depression because of the stressful demands of living with a person who suffers from schizophrenia. According to the survey, 77 percent of caregivers said they played an "extremely important role" in the treatment of the schizophrenic person. Moreover, about 80 percent of the caregivers claimed that health care professionals did not understand the problems faced by family members.

Because the person with mental illness can become the focus of the family—as everyone attempts to keep appointments, adjust schedules, and make allowances—family members may come to feel ignored and resentful. They may need to set aside private time to pursue their own interests. The primary caregiver, moreover, needs to schedule time to rest. Sometimes, in difficult or long-term cases, family members should seek counseling themselves.

Above all, keeping problems in perspective is the key to coping with the effects of mental illness. Most people with mental illness can and do get the disorder under control and resume productive lives.

APPENDIX

FOR MORE INFORMATION

The following national organizations are dedicated to increasing awareness of mental health issues and providing information to people with mental health problems.

American Academy of Child and Adolescent Psychiatry
3615 Wisconsin Avenue, NW
Washington, DC 20016-3007
(202) 966-7300
http://www.aacap.org/

American Psychiatric Association
1400 K Street, NW
Washington, DC 20005
(202) 682-6000
http://www.psych.org/

American Psychological Association
750 First Street, NE
Washington, DC 20002
(202) 336-5500
http://www.apa.org/

Anxiety Disorders Association of America (ADAA)
11900 Parklawn Drive, Suite 100
Rockville, MD 20852
(301) 231-9350

Canadian Mental Health Association (CMHA)
2160 Yonge Street, 3d Floor
Toronto, Ontario M4S 2Z3
Canada
(416) 484-7750
http://www.cmha.ca/

Children and Adults with Attention Deficit Disorders (CHADD)
499 N.W. Seventieth Avenue
Suite 101
Plantation, FL 33317
(954) 587-3700

Council for Children with Behavioral Disorders
Council for Exceptional Children
1920 Association Drive
Reston, VA 20191-1589
(703) 264-9446
http://www.cec.sped.org/

Knowledge Exchange Network (KEN)
Center for Mental Health Services
P.O. Box 42490
Washington, DC 20015
(800) 789-2647
E-mail: ken@mentalhealth.org
http://www.mentalhealth.org/

National Alliance for the Mentally Ill
200 North Glebe Road, Suite 1015
Arlington, VA 22203-3754
(703) 524-7600
(800) 950-6264
http://www.nami.org/

National Depressive and Manic-Depressive Association
730 N. Franklin Street
Suite 501
Chicago, IL 60610
(312) 642-7243

National Institute of Mental Health (NIMH)
NIMH Public Inquiries
6001 Executive Boulevard
Room 8184 MSC 9663
Bethesda, MD 20892-9663
(301) 443-4513
E-mail: nimhinfo@nih.gov
http://www.nimh.nih.gov/

National Mental Health Association
1021 Prince Street
Alexandria, VA 22314-2971
(703) 684-7722
(800) 969-6642
http://www.nmha.org/

Obsessive Compulsive Foundation (OCF)
P.O. Box 70
Milford, CT 06460-0070
(203) 878-5669

APPENDIX

BIBLIOGRAPHY

American Psychiatric Association. *Diagnostic and Statistical Manual of Mental Disorders,* 4th ed. Washington, D.C.: American Psychiatric Association, 1994.

———. *Let's Talk Facts About Mental Illnesses: An Overview,* revised ed. Washington, D.C.: American Psychiatric Association, 1997.

———. "Mental Health Parity: Its Time Has Come." In *APA Online: Public Policy Advocacy* (April 1999) [online]. Available at <http://www.psych. org/psych/htdocs/Pub_Pol_adv/fac-parity.html>. Accessed August 1999.

———. "Psychiatric Effects of Media Violence." APA Fact Sheet Series. In *APA Online: Public Information* [online]. Available at <http://www.psych. org/psych/htdocs/public_info/media_violence.html>. Accessed August 1999.

———. "Violence and Mental Illness." APA Fact Sheet Series. In *APA Online: Public Information* [online]. Available at <http://www.psych.org/public_ info/violen~1.htm>. Accessed September 1999.

American Psychological Association. "The Effectiveness of Psychological Services in Improving Employee Productivity and Attendance." Practice Directorate. Washington, D.C., June 1992.

Baulk, Catherine. "Why Isn't Mental Illness Talked About?" In *First Person* [online]. Available at <http://www.vulliamy.demon.co.uk/>. Accessed September 1999.

Bellenir, Karen, ed. *Mental Health Disorders Sourcebook.* Detroit: Omni-graphics, 1996.

Brink, Susan. "I'll Say I'm Suicidal." *U.S. News and World Report,* 19 January 1998, 63.

Carver, Deborah. "Workplace Violence." Report of a presentation by Phillip Resnick, M.D., at the U.S. Psychiatric and Mental Health Congress, San Diego, California, November 16, 1996 [online]. Available at <http://www. medscape.com/>. Accessed August 1999.

Cockerham, William C. *Sociology of Mental Disorder,* 5th ed. Upper Saddle River, N.J.: Prentice Hall, 2000.

Duke, Patty, and Kenneth Turan. *Call Me Anna: The Autobiography of Patty Duke.* New York: Bantam Doubleday Dell, 1988.

Dwyer, Kevin, David Osher, et al. *Early Warning, Timely Response: A Guide to Safe Schools: The Referenced Edition.* Washington, D.C.: American Institutes for Research, 1998.

Dykstra, Tracey. "How I Cope." *Schizophrenia Bulletin* 23, no.4 (1997): 697–99.

"Employee Assistance Programs." Program Policy. University of Texas, Austin, 17 May 1989.

"Family Shroud for the Mentally Ill." *Science News,* 7 March 1998, 152.

Gabbard, Glen O. "Are All Psychotherapies Equally Effective?" *Menninger Letter* 3 (1995): 1–2.

Holm, Emma. "Colder Weather." In *First Person* [online]. Available at <http://www.vulliamy.demon.co.uk/>. Accessed September 1999.

Kemp, Mark. "Out of the Woods." *Rolling Stone,* 11 December 1997.

Kleinfield, N. R., and Kit R. Roane. "Subway Killing Casts Light on Suspect's Mental Torment." *New York Times,* 11 January 1999.

Menninger, Roy W. "Reducing TV Violence May Curb Antisocial Behavior." *Menninger Letter* 3 (1995): 4–5.

"Mental Health: Does Therapy Work?" *Consumer Reports,* November 1995, 734–39.

Murphy, Marcia A. "First Person Account: Meaning of Psychoses." *Schizophrenia Bulletin* 23, no.3 (1997): 541–43.

National Alliance for the Mentally Ill. "Myths vs. Facts About Mental Illness." Arlington, Virginia [online]. Available at <http://www.nami.org/cgi-bin/wwwais.cgi>. Accessed December 1998.

National Coalition for the Homeless. "Mental Illness and Homelessness." NCH Fact Sheet #5. Washington, D.C., October 1997.

National Institute of Mental Health. "The Numbers Count: Mental Illness in America." NIH Publication No. NIH 99-4584. Bethesda, Maryland, 1999.

National Mental Health Association. "Did You Know?" NMHA Information Center, Alexandria, Virginia [online]. Available at <http://www.nmha.org/infoctr/didyou.cfm>. Accessed September 1999.

O'Connor, Herb J. "The Cleavers Don't Live Here Anymore: Some Schools Are Facing Up to Their Students' Mental Health Problems." In *ABCNEWS.com* [online]. Available at <http://abcnews.go.com/>. Accessed 20 May 1999.

Peele, Stanton, and Richard DeGrandpre. "My Genes Made Me Do It." *Psychology Today,* July/August 1995.

Powell, Jackie. "First Person Account: Paranoid Schizophrenia—A Daughter's Story." *Schizophrenia Bulletin* 24, no. 1 (1998): 175–76.

Rouse, Beatrice A., ed. *Statistics Source Book, 1998.* Washington, D.C.: Substance Abuse and Mental Health Services Administration, 1998.

Schazberg, Alan F., and Charles B. Nemeroff, eds. *The American Psychiatric Textbook of Psychopharmacology.* Washington, D.C.: American Psychiatric Press, 1995.

Schiller, Lori, and Amanda Bennett. *Quiet Room: A Journey Out of the Torment.* New York: Warner, 1996.

SerVass, Cory. "The *Post* Investigates Manic-Depression." *Saturday Evening Post,* March/April 1996.

"Study Shows Depression Prevalent Among Schizophrenia Caregivers." *Mental Health Weekly* 8, no. 32 (17 August 1998).

"Survey: Stigma Keeps Millions with Anxiety Disorders from Treatment." In *Mental Health Net,* November 5, 1998 [online]. Available at <http://mentalhelp.net/articles/anxiety51.htm>.

"Two-Thirds of Psychiatric Hospitals Dump Patients for Economic Reasons." *Mental Health Net,* December 9, 1997 [online]. Available at <http://mentalhelp.net/articles/dumping.htm>.

"Video Offers Help and Hope for People with Mental Illness." *Carter Center News* (Atlanta), Summer 1996.

"What Do People Know About Mental Illness?" *USA Today,* December 1997, 9.

White House Conference on Mental Health. "Myths and Facts About Mental Illness," June 7, 1999 [online]. Available at <http://www.mentalhealth.gov/myths.asp>. Accessed July 1999.

Yanson, J. "The 1991 National Executive Poll on Health Care Costs and Benefits." *Business and Health,* September 1991, 61–71.

APPENDIX

FURTHER READING

Carter, Rosalynn, with Susan K. Golant. *Helping Someone with Mental Illness.* New York: Times Books, 1999.

Dinner, Sherry H. *Nothing to Be Ashamed Of: Growing Up with Mental Illness in Your Family.* New York: Lothrop, Lee and Shepard, 1989.

Folkers, Gladys, and Jeanne Engelmann. *Taking Charge of My Mind and Body: A Girls' Guide to Outsmarting Alcohol, Drugs, Smoking, and Eating Problems.* Minneapolis: Free Spirit, 1997.

Hyde, Margaret O., and Elizabeth H. Forsyth. *Know About Mental Illness.* New York: Walker, 1996.

Johnson, Julie Tallard. *Understanding Mental Illness.* Flushing, N.Y.: Lerner, 1990.

Klebanoff, Susan, and Ellen Luborsky. *Ups and Downs: How to Beat the Blues and Teen Depression.* New York: Prince Stern, 1999.

Krulik, Nancy E. *Don't Stress! How to Keep Life's Problems Little.* New York: Scholastic, 1998.

McCoy, Kathy, and Charles Wibbelsman. *Life Happens: A Teenager's Guide to Friends, Failure, Sexuality, Love, Rejection, Addiction, Peer Pressure, Families, Loss, Depression, Change, and Other Challenges of Living.* New York: Perigee, 1996.

Quinn, Patricia O., and Judith Stern. *Putting on the Brakes: Young Person's Guide to Understanding Attention Deficit Disorder.* Washington: Magination, 1992.

Roukema, Richard. *What Every Patient, Family, Friend, and Caregiver Needs to Know About Psychiatry.* Washington, D.C.: American Psychiatric Press, 1998.

Sanders, Pete, and Steve Meyers. *Depression and Mental Health.* Brookfield, Conn.: Copper Beech, 1998.

APPENDIX

GLOSSARY

Anorexia nervosa: an eating disorder, affecting mainly young women, that is characterized by a distorted body image and an intense desire to lose an excessive amount of weight.

Anxiety disorder: a category of mental disorders in which the primary symptoms are excessive fears or anxieties, often manifested in panic attacks; the category includes generalized anxiety disorder as well as phobias, panic disorder, obsessive-compulsive disorder, and posttraumatic stress disorder.

Attention-deficit/hyperactivity disorder: a psychological disorder, occurring mainly in children and adolescents, characterized by prominent symptoms of inattention and/or impulsivity.

Bipolar disorder: a mood disorder characterized by serious episodes of depression alternating with manic feelings.

Bulimia nervosa: an eating disorder, primarily affecting young women, marked by a cycle of consuming large amounts of food and then vomiting, using laxatives, or taking other inappropriate measures to prevent weight gain.

Delusion: a false belief maintained by a person despite obvious evidence to the contrary.

Depression: a mental state characterized by feelings of sadness, hopelessness, and lack of interest in life; for persistent or severe depression, specialists use a number of specific categories, such as major depressive disorder.

Hallucination: a condition in which a person has a sensory perception (usually involving sight, hearing, or smell) of something that is not actually present.

Mania: excessive feelings of power, excitement, elation, and accelerated thinking and speaking.

Mood disorder: a category of mental disorders in which the primary symptom is a disturbance in the patient's mood; the category includes bipolar disorder and depressive disorders.

Neurotransmitters: chemicals used to transmit messages between nerve cells in the brain; problems with neurotransmitters are believed to be a cause of many mental illnesses.

Panic attack: intense fear or discomfort that begins suddenly, builds quickly to a peak, and is accompanied by such symptoms as trembling, heart palpitations, dizziness, sweating, shortness of breath, and the sensation of smothering.

Panic disorder: recurrent, unexpected panic attacks accompanied by worry about them or by other behavioral changes.

Phobia: persistent, irrational fear of an object, activity, or situation.

Psychotic disorder: a serious mental disturbance, such as schizophrenia, that interferes with a person's thinking, perceiving, and making rational choices.

Psychotherapy: "talk" therapy in which a patient and therapist discuss the patient's feelings, behaviors, and problems and how to change them in desirable ways.

Schizophrenia: a psychosis that causes people to have a distorted sense of reality, as evidenced by such symptoms as delusions and hallucinations.

APPENDIX

INDEX

APPENDIX

PICTURE CREDITS

page

8: Otto Dix (1891–1969), *The Madwoman* (1925), Staedtische Kunsthalle, Mannheim, Germany; Erich Lessing/Art Resource, N.Y.

10: David De Lossy/The Image Bank, 1999

12: AP/Wide World Photos

15: Urban Archives, Philadelphia

18: © David M. Grossman/Photo Researchers

20: Steve Niedorf/The Image Bank, 1998

22: © Ed Lettau/Photo Researchers

23: Archive Photos

25: © Susan Rosenberg/Photo Researchers

28: AP/Wide World Photos

30: Telemaco Signorini (1835–1901), *The Ward of the Insane at San Bonifacio, Florence* (1865), Galleria d'Arte Moderna, Venice, Italy; Scala/Art Resource, N.Y.

33: Archive Photos

34: Archive Photos

37: Archive Photos

38: Archive Photos

40: AP/Wide World Photos

42: © Telegraph Colour Library/FPG International LLC

45: Alan Danaher/The Image Bank, 1998

49: AP/Wide World Photos

52: AP/Wide World Photos

54: Archive Photos

57: AP/Wide World Photos

58: © Jim Cummins/FPG International LLC

62: © Michael Hart/FPG International LLC

66: © Jeff Baker/FPG International LLC

68: HMS Images/The Image Bank, 1996

70: AP/WideWorld Photos

74: © Stephen Simpson/FPG International LLC

75: Suzanne Opton/The Image Bank, 1998

77: AP/Wide World Photos

78: © Joseph Sohm; ChromoSohm Inc./Corbis

81: Anne Rippy/The Image Bank, 1999

82: © Shirley Zeiberg

86: Real Life/The Image Bank, 1994

Senior Consulting Editor Carol C. Nadelson, M.D., is president and chief executive officer of the American Psychiatric Press, Inc., staff physician at Cambridge Hospital, and Clinical Professor of Psychiatry at Harvard Medical School. In addition to her work with the American Psychiatric Association, which she served as vice president in 1981–83 and president in 1985–86, Dr. Nadelson has been actively involved in other major psychiatric organizations, including the Group for the Advancement of Psychiatry, the American College of Psychiatrists, the Association for Academic Psychiatry, the American Association of Directors of Psychiatric Residency Training Programs, the American Psychosomatic Society, and the American College of Mental Health Administrators. In addition, she has been a consultant to the Psychiatric Education Branch of the National Institute of Mental Health and has served on the editorial boards of several journals. Doctor Nadelson has received many awards, including the Gold Medal Award for significant and ongoing contributions in the field of psychiatry, the Elizabeth Blackwell Award for contributions to the causes of women in medicine, and the Distinguished Service Award from the American College of Psychiatrists for outstanding achievements and leadership in the field of psychiatry.

Consulting Editor Claire E. Reinburg, M.A., is editorial director of the American Psychiatric Press, Inc., which publishes about 60 new books and six journals a year. She is a graduate of Georgetown University in Washington, D.C., where she earned bachelor of arts and master of arts degrees in English. She is a member of the Council of Biology Editors, the Women's National Book Association, the Society for Scholarly Publishing, and Washington Book Publishers.

Charles Shields was formerly the chairman of the guidance department at Homewood-Flossmoor High School in Flossmoor, Illinois. He currently writes full-time from his home in Homewood, Illinois, where he lives with his wife, Guadalupe, an elementary school principal.